101 WAYS TO KILL YOUR BOSS

101 WAYS TO KILL YOUR BOSS

GRAHAM ROUMIEU

headline

First published in 2007
by HEADLINE PUBLISHING GROUP

3

Cataloguing in Publication Data is available from the British Library

ISBN 978 0 7553 1688 5

Typeset by Avon DataSet Ltd, Bidford-on-Avon, Warwickshire

Printed and bound in Great Britain by Butler & Tanner

Headline's policy is to use papers that are natural, renewable and recyclable products and made from wood grown in sustainable forests. The logging and manufacturing processes are expected to conform to the environmental regulations of the country of origin.

HEADLINE PUBLISHING GROUP
An Hachette Livre UK Company
338 Euston Road
London NW1 3BH

www.headline.co.uk
www.hodderheadline.com

For Dad

ROTU-
CLEANER

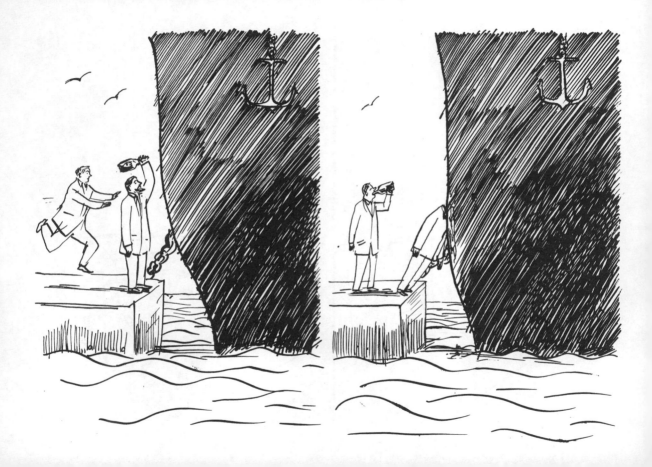

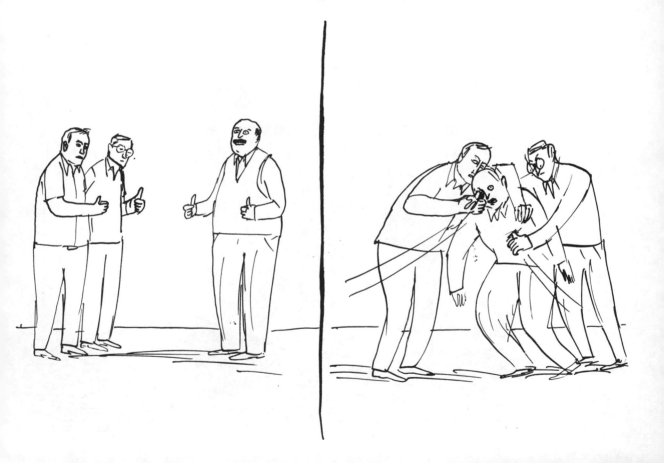

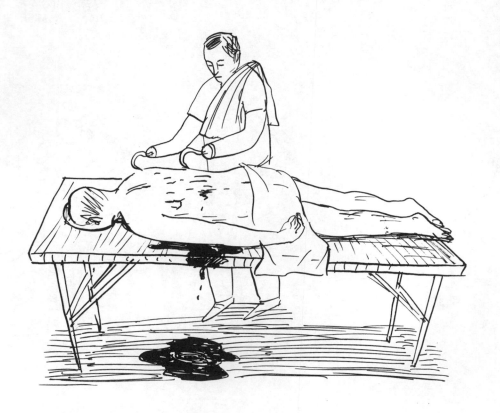

HAPPY RETIREMENT

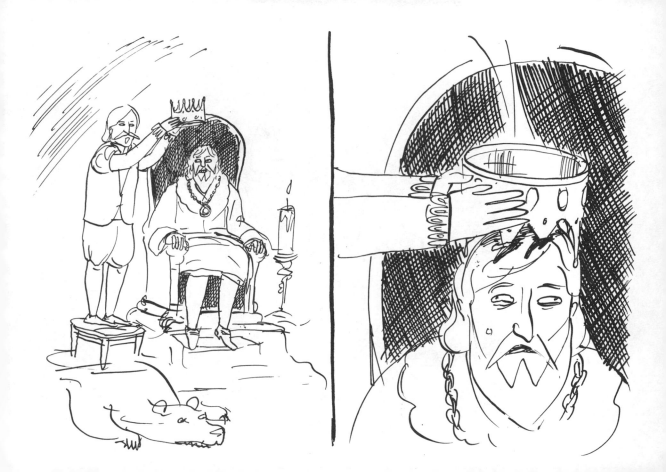

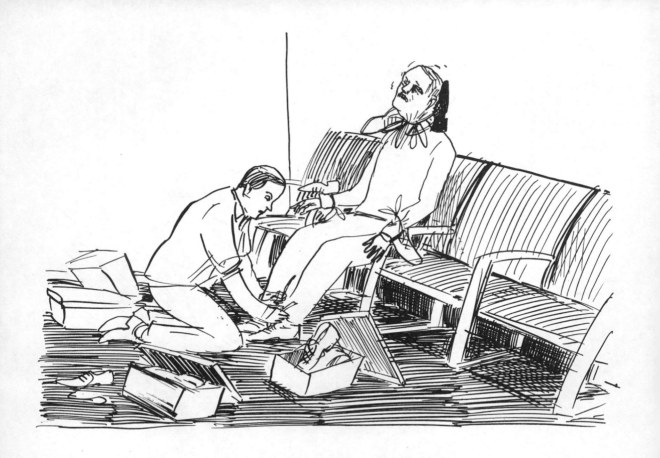

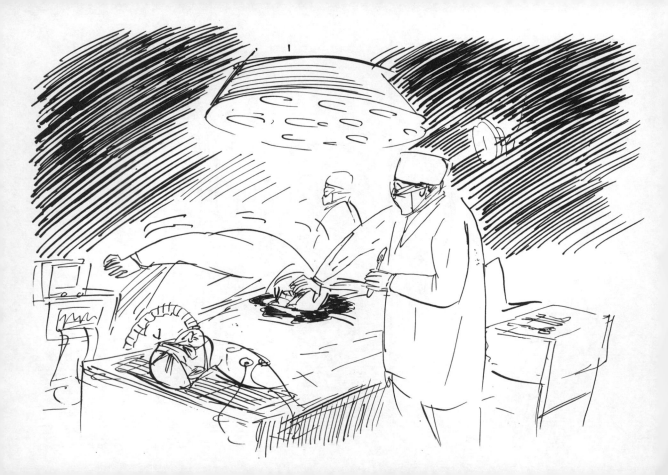

It's A New World After All
Michelle Marie Engel

Second Edition, 2008
Limited Edition Printing

Published in the U.S.
Michelle Marie Engel
Visionary Solutions

To order more books visit:
www.visionarysolutions.org

Or write to Michelle at:
michelle@visionarysolutions.org

ISBN: 978-1-934332-07-8

Cover Design by
André Angermann
www.livinglightcreations.com
541-488-9639
Ashland, Oregon

Layout and printing in the U.S. by
Interactive Media Publishing
PO Box 1407
Phoenix, OR 97535
541-535-5552
www.i-mediapub.com

Dedication

To my grandmother, Myrta Newark
For leading by example
For unconditional love
For believing in me

To my son, Jason Alan Engel
For your love, wisdom, and encouragement
For growing into such a fine man—21 years at the printing of this Second Edition
I am very proud of who you are and your loving and creative expressions

To my love, Bruce
For your continuing support
For your love and companionship
And for making it possible to focus on my life's work

To all of you pioneering souls who are expressing your Divine Essence,
God's perfect love, to create Heaven on Earth.
I believe in you.

Gary,
Your kindness
has touched my
heart deeply.
Thank you so
much, you are sweet!
Love,
Michelle

Forward

This book was begun in my early twenties as I contemplated life in writing with poems such as "The Destiny of Every Man is Death" and "Being Human." Over the years, I increasingly gained insights through the synthesis of meditation, contemplation, reading, and life experiences. Most of the time, I was just writing for the fulfillment of my own self-expression. It was not originally intended that I would bare my soul to the public with my inner musings.

As I have evolved and grown into a more authentic and loving being, I did decide to let my soul stand naked with confidence because I realized that deep down, we are all the same. We may not all think the same way or feel the same way at any given moment, or at any particular level of evolution, but certainly, the more we become Self-realized, the more we emulate the purity of our Essence from our common Source and sense our Oneness of Spirit.

We do all have the same types of feelings. We do all pursue happiness in our own way. And it seems to me, we are all awakening right now. I notice lots of people going through the same types of things: same changes, same fears, same lessons, same insights, same hopes, and same dreams.

Somehow I've captured some insights and processes, and an understanding of certain phenomena that sheds some light on the awakening process. My experience on the outside may look different from yours, but on the inside it is the same process.

I've also noticed the Universal Vision that is emerging. Each person that consciously tunes in to their heart begins to find what brings them joy; they get a picture of what their dreams are made of. Some people's visions are more expansive than others in scope. But what is really becoming evident is that by blending all of our dreams and visions into one, we glimpse the Universal Vision of the Divine Plan. We see what our life purpose is in the fulfillment of God's Plan to create a world of peace, love, joy, and abundance for all. We all have a piece, and we need each other.

When we totally master our personal energy through self-awareness and conscious direction of consciousness, we change the consciousness of the world. When the scale is tipped in the favor of the new consciousness, then an amazing global shift will occur. The disturbing circumstances on our planet will no longer exist. They will be replaced with the new energy of loving cooperation, and all will benefit.

Part of my contribution is to share some understanding that will aid many who are going through the shift at this time. I am also fully aware that my energy comes along with the words on the pages of this book. I am here with you now. What I have gained at the level of consciousness, I am intentionally sharing with you energetically.

Truth feels good. Only take within you that which feels good to your own soul. Love feels good. Know that love reveals the truth and the truth reveals love. If you wish to feel good, you can use love in any moment to transform anything that doesn't feel good into truth. Then you can express this truth and feel good again. You will be free.

The purpose of It's A New World After All is to demonstrate that we are all on the same page when we live from our hearts. I have faith that we will stand united in truth and integrity and bring Heaven to Earth in this new era of peace and joy.

It IS a New World after all—it's already here—and the global expansion is inevitable. This is the time to unite, celebrate, and lovingly cooperate as we work to fulfill our life missions.

Acknowledgements

I feel deep gratitude for all of my family and friends who believe in me and have helped me survive under the most trying times. With their compassion and their willingness to help and share, it enabled me to persevere and follow my dreams and my passion of service to the world.

A huge thank you to Helene Enslow for her editing efforts for the Second Edition of It's A New World After All.

I appreciate Trish Wiggins and Bob Worrell for showing up for me with amazingly generous gifts and actions over such a long period of time and continuously caring for my welfare with love and generosity that surpasses normal human capacity—they are angels.

I will be forever grateful to: my brother, David Barks, my sister, Carolyn Wilson, and my grandmother and spiritual mentor, Myrta Newark. Loving gratitude to my parents, Robert and Bonnie Yager. And to all my beautiful friends: Joe Collier, Marion Assenmacher, Ellen James, Susan Campbell, Jim Dreaver, Ed Barr, Desiree Palermo, Amanda Mowery, Twila Batie, Deborah Delaunay, Libby McGeorge-Kester, Armando Busick, Larry Frires, André Angermann, Jim Bowne, Marianne Weidlein, William Cerf, Daniel Blake, Ed Keller, and David Om.

A special thanks to my son, Jason Engel, who has been my teacher in so many ways: always patient, encouraging, calming, never complaining about sacrifices, always offering magnificent ideas and insights about my life or what I could do next, and especially for his deep concern for my well-being—asking me if I'm all right, and always telling me that things would work out. He has become an independent man of amazing creativity and authenticity. I am so very proud of him.

Deep heartfelt gratitude to my love, Bruce Petko, for loving me, helping me, supporting me, and providing the means to finally have my first book published. Right when the chips seemed to be the most down, Bruce came along as an answer to a prayer and delivered God's love with flying rainbow colors. I will always appreciate his bundle of blessings.

These people are evidence of the energy of compassion, cooperation, understanding, and love in action—the best security we have in our New World. May all of their love and compassion come back to them a thousandfold while they experience their spiritual evolution of fully realizing their true Selves, and experiencing all of their deepest hearts' desires as all of their dreams miraculously come true.

I am truly blessed by God, who shows up in all of these forms.

I am truly, deeply, forever grateful.

All my purest love, Michelle

How to Best Benefit from
It's A New World After All

A Note From Michelle...

The message contained in this literature is from my heart to yours. I would like to request that you breathe deeply and get centered before you read and then listen with your heart. It may be beneficial to space out the reading, since there is quite a bit here and some of it warrants some deep contemplation.

You may notice that this is a book based on expanding concepts. There are 44 topics, each with the word, a quote, a poem, and an essay. This is a great book to open to any page and find your perfect message in the moment. You may wish to read just the page, or the quote, poem, and essay from that topic.

It may also be of value to look up a concept that has been synchronistically popping into your awareness. If you hear something three times or more, it's time to look into it! Also, you may be experiencing a shift in your life that can be nurtured by an understanding of its phenomenon expressed in one of the topics. Lastly, by re-reading some of these messages, you may find an even deeper message, or pick up on something that was not evident the first time you read it.

It's A New World After All contains inspirational messages of truth and love. It describes what is happening in the world right now, mostly behind the scenes. We are opening to a new reality based on feelings and personal empowerment. My intention is to provide messages that help us to realize how much we are the same and how connected we are to each other. In doing so, I hope to help improve your life and our world.

Namaste!
Michelle Marie Engel

Other Books by **Michelle Engel**

Life Inspired

Stories for Awakened Awareness I

Clothing of the Soul
Nothing But Angels
A God's Eye View
Finding Soul's Passion
Sir Laughalot
You Are Special
The Value of Love
Axes for Taxes
A Peace of Gratitude
My Heart is Smart
I Love Green Eggs and Ham, I AM That I AM
Bee Love

Stories for Awakened Awareness II

Rise Above with Love
Being Real
A Case of Mistaken Identity
The Hammer of Humility
Reflect on Respect
Forgiveness
The Truth Fairy
Nurturing Self-Love
Choice Point
I Rest My Faith
Let's Go Fishing
Take A Stand

Stories for Awakened Awareness III

Help Me Walk the Talk
Why You Have Nothing
Everything's Going to be All Light

Image
Sincerity
Soul to Soul
The Wizard of Is
Belief Barbecue
Mastering Divinity: Perception to Expression
Boundaries for Bullies
Gentle Evolution
The Great Giver

Stories for Awakened Awareness IV

Compassion
Overcome
Isness is My Business
The Evolution Revolution
Surrender

AND...

I  Opener Reminder Cards

INSPIRATIONAL CREATIONS: Unique Framed Poetry & Quote Art Gifts!

Beautifully decorated and framed poetry and quote art that include favorite poems and quotes from **It's A New World After All** and other inspirational literature by Michelle are available at:

Linda's Unique Creations
21901 Hwy 62 Suite A
Shady Cove, Oregon

For more information visit: www.visionarysolutions.org
Or contact Michelle at: michelle@visionarysolutions.org
Mailing address: Michelle Engel
P.O. Box 247
Shady Cove, OR 97539

Table of Contents

Love

"Love one another."

Jesus Christ

Love's Team

If you would like to live your dream
Here's an invitation to join Love's Team
It's your energy that helps tilt the world toward peace
The direction of your attention can make love increase

Look inside right down to your core
Feel the love and love your Self more
Sparkles of your energy intermingle with the whole
Your compassion is powerful as you radiate your soul

Love's Team is now strengthening and growing
As we each surrender to Life and join with its flowing
The joy that we feel creates a life of ease
We realize we can create whatever we please

What pleases you? Have you thought lately?
Do what you love and increase your joy greatly
Imagine your job in this life that you live
Is just to make your Self happy by all that you give

Since we're all One love flows all ways
Loving your Self brightens all of our days
And when we love others by being kind
We love our whole Self, we're no longer blind

Welcome to Love's Team, your energy is flowing
Your soul is shining brightly, really—you're glowing!
We've bonded so sweetly in our new vibration
It's a global love that's uniting every nation

Turn Up the Love!!

We are at a critical juncture in human evolution. The ultimate truth is that it is time to tune in to love and turn up its expression in the world. We are receiving Divine help right now in a big way. If you are in a panic or feel unsettled, you are not tuned in. If you observe the chaos of people's lives and world conditions and still feel a sense of peace, you are tuned in. If you are feeling a complete sense of peace, joy, and harmony as you complete your life's mission while being consistently kind and cooperating with others, you are already living in our New World.

As awakening souls, we are all up against some pretty tough life choices. Our Universal intention as souls is to choose love as our motivation in every moment. It goes beyond that, though. We are no longer choosing from either/or options. We are embracing the paradoxical nature of unity consciousness. This awareness encompasses both aspects of being separate people and part of the whole life system of unified spirit.

Internal unity is accomplished when we tune in to the deepest part of our consciousness in our hearts and blend this inherent love wisdom with our conscious minds. We absolve the confusion of our hearts saying one thing and our minds saying another. We feel a deep sense of certainty. Love from our heart is our Source of being and illuminates the truth with Light. The separated mind seems lost in its vast array of infinite possibilities until it is reconciled with our heart to know truth. Within the mind, the imagination becomes the laboratory of manifestation when it is open to receive and perceive the truth. As the mind surrenders to love, the female and male energies are integrated and harmonized to effortlessly flow in the conscious participation of Life. The energy of Life always follows the Laws of Love.

When it comes to love, we are realizing how we can accept and love others just the way they are without compromising ourselves. After all, Jesus said "love others as thyself" implying that we are to love ourselves as well as we love others. There's an equation there that signifies the balance we are seeking.

We can love ourselves the best by first delving inside and making a secure connection with God, our Source of love and life. God loves us each deeply, unconditionally. We can place our attention into our hearts and really feel it. By remaining tuned in to our core, the fire of Divinity in our hearts, we receive the full knowing of our True Selves. We know we are love. We feel our feelings and we honor them as messengers of Truth. When we love our own feelings, we stay connected to Truth and Love, the nature of God and our own true nature. By communicating our feelings honestly to God, our own pure spark of God inside our hearts, without denial or self-judgment, we love ourselves unconditionally and feel God's unconditional love. The more we experience God's unconditional love in our personal, still moments, the more we can turn up the love in our life in terms of its expression to ourselves and others. We realize in full experience our Oneness with All That Is. This is the key to reaching our Highest Destiny.

Turning up the love with full expression feels good to everyone. By being forgiving, accepting, understanding, compassionate, kind, and appreciative to our inner Self and others, we are cooperating in the Divine Plan. Just imagine how good life feels when we treat ourselves and every other individual as precious and highly valuable. Just imagine what life would feel like if everyone followed what brings them joy in their hearts, and just shared joy and laughter and love as the energy underpinning all of life's experiences. Just imagine a feeling of security and inner peace with the full knowing that love and faith in our innermost Self creates a peaceful, joyous, harmonious world.

What if we start by making a choice to treat ourselves well? We can understand ourselves and forgive ourselves faster and faster for perceived wrongdoings. We can feel the joy of our Inner Child emerge as we begin to play, have fun, and create. We can comfort ourselves by creating bubble baths or walks in nature. We can treat ourselves to whatever it is that we, personally, enjoy the most. What have you done for yourself lately? How often do you do things just to make yourself feel good? Do you realize, precious one, that by making yourself feel good, you help the world? You really do.

We feel good when we express love, whether it is to ourselves, or others. Other people are really part of our whole Self. Our growth period is about noticing, understanding, and fully embracing our Oneness in Spirit. Spirit is electromagnetic energy. Energetically, we are literally all connected. We have always "sensed" things about each other that were unspoken. When that energy is in our space, it becomes part of us. We exchange energy all the time because we really are one energetic life system. Now we realize, when we love another, we truly are loving another aspect of our self—we love our Whole Self.

Let's understand that everyone does their very best in life and that we each deserve a lot of compassion. Let's enjoy our new energy of peaceful cooperation and creative inspiration. Let's appreciate each other and show it. When it comes to each choice that we make in our behavior, let's make sure it comes from loving energy. Let's express the pure love that we are.

It is a New World after all. We are accessing and expressing more and more love, and we feel good!! Let's continue to turn up the love.

Inheritance

"But the meek shall inherit the earth,
and shall delight themselves in the abundance of peace."

Psalm 37:11

Inheritance

It seems as though we're weak at times
When we go inside to dwell
But that is where our true strength lies
It's not our outer shell

The times I feel the strongest
Is often when I cry
Because then I go right to our Source
And strength wells up inside

I feel God's love pour through me
Soothing me through my soul
And expressing it to others
Is now my only goal

So many of us dwell inside
Enough now we can say
The changing of the guard
Is surely on its way

Look at all the misery
We're creating here on earth
It doesn't have to be that way
We need new vision first

A vision powered by love
Seeing what we can create
Shifting internal consciousness
Opening heaven's gate

Of all of God's great creatures
The strength comes from the meek
Who now shall inherit the Earth
Providing answers we all seek

Dedicated to the Inner Strength in you!

My Cup Runneth Over

Love is all we really need in life. It's all we really want deep down. It's also what we are deep down. We are what we are in our hearts.

We are just like Dorothy in the Wizard of Oz. Everything we're searching for is with us all the time. When we find that place within, we have all of the attributes that the scarecrow, the tin man, and the lion are searching for. We are the essence of God, complete with wisdom, love, and courage. The scarecrow thought he had to find wisdom outside of himself, so he was in search for a brain. The tin man thought he was missing a heart, but his essence of love was already present. The lion felt he needed courage, but despite his fears, he stood his ground in what he believed. This essence welled up from inside when push came to shove and he just didn't realize at first that it was there all along. Dorothy just wanted to go home. She realized all she had to do was place her attention on home as she held that desire in her heart--and there she was. Dorothy was home in her heart.

When we delve inside and drink from the cup of life, we realize we have an abundance of life, of love, and of everything we could possibly desire. This is God—the alpha and omega. The beginning and the end of ourselves, our life, and everything in creation. It's the stuff we are made of and the stuff we create with.

"Seek ye first the kingdom of God, and everything else shall be added unto you." When we put these words into action, we no longer search for what we desire outside of us. We go to God, our Source. We are comforted and loved. We feel completely fulfilled and receive all the Source energy we need to create the fulfillment of all of our desires.

There's nothing so simple as to just sit and be with God. It feels like a soul bath...so refreshing. I recorded one particularly sweet communion that I will share with you here. I know that you have had your own. It is so natural. In these times, we need to return here often to acquire our most valuable assets of courage, wisdom, and love and apply them in our lives individually and our world together.

Being Present With God...

Showing up as an innocent child, a soul who is seeking to understand life and live it most beneficially and successfully, is the way I've learned that I can be present with God. Going into my heart and being real, really delving in and exploring my deepest feelings brings me very close to God: I feel our Oneness, I sense at the very deepest level God's love for me. When I get present with God, it brings me to tears. I feel such a deep and fulfilling love. It fills me up not only in the moment, but for a long, long time. In a way, it changes me forever.

I just had such an experience. I took all of my concerns, questions, feelings, and desires to God with an open heart. I left with a deep sense of knowingness that God heard me, is always with me, and that I will feel the joy and love and peace throughout my outer life as well. I always know this, but when I have deep inner experiences with God, it deepens the senses and shifts my consciousness ever closer to a lasting experience of cosmic consciousness and bliss. I don't just think that everything is divinely perfect, but I realize it and sense it in every aspect of my being—I know it in my heart. It's like thinking about what hot chocolate tastes like as opposed to the direct of experience of drinking it, tasting the yummy-ness of it while smelling its chocolaty aroma, and feeling it go down your throat and warm your belly.

During these moments I behold the most wonderfully awesome communion with God. I pour out all my questions. I receive perfectly divine answers. I release through my tears all of the pent up energy of anything lacking or unfulfilling in my life. I think of how I am and how I choose to be, knowing that God supports me 100%. I feel and express my deep gratitude. I am clear and free and I'm ready to purely understand and express who I truly am. I feel light and joyous. I know that I am love and I'm ready to go out and express it ever more fully in the world.

I love God so much. My only aim in life is to be Self-realized, to be God-Like in every way, expressing the pure natural unique essence of my True Self. I intend to love myself unconditionally and to love others unconditionally as well, as I somehow benefit them with my beingness.

Just like a bird sucking sweet nectar, I will always go back for more. I remember I always have. It feels so good.

Empowerment

Empowerment is just a matter of realizing
and expressing our True Selves.

Victims Become Creators

Victimization once perceived
Clearly illusions, now relieved
Empowered by soul; nature unfolds
New story now to be told

Each life is impacting
'Tis the universe reacting
Sparks of soul igniting
Passion, expression uniting

Consciously creating, essence of soul
Being inwardly, outwardly whole
Harmonizing with All That Is
Deep sensation of being this

Power of consciousness is the key
Changes within individually
Personal impact realization
Upon total world, every nation

Creating with vision, feelings of heart
New World experience; this is the start
Energy of compassion, tool to create
World, wake up—don't hesitate!

A New Perspective

Life is full of lessons. Most of them are personal or group lessons, but there was a message to the entire world on September 11, 2001. In its most simple form, the message said "Wake Up!"

Because of the mass destruction and loss of lives, the majority of the world's population was sent directly to the depths of our hearts to feel compassion. The whole energy in the world shifted that day.

At once we felt a bond of unity with our brothers and sisters in their suffering. Many of us had realizations about life that shook us out of our mindsets and lifestyles that changed us forever. We began looking at life with a broader perspective.

We are not victims. The highest level of our beings, the Spirit of our soul, creates these circumstances for our benefit. The people in our lives are experiencing the same thing: challenges from which to grow. Hopefully, as we realize this, we can develop a continual nature of compassion for ourselves, and each other.

For myself, the application of this realization has set me free in many ways. It has also cascaded into many other realizations that make me feel more and more compassion, love, and gratitude and less and less disturbance in my heart and in my mind. We are learning that by creating peace in our own inner sanctuary and in our lives, we are creating peace in the world.

The new energy in the world has caused us to unleash all of our old pent up feelings: pains and scars from the past. We're edgy. Our buttons get pushed. We feel instant karma, things are happening to us that show signs of what a reflection life is. We are changing rapidly in this new energy. We are becoming more humble and expressing our true nature of love.

As we move our attention to the global situation, we see people who seem to be entertaining ill intention and doing things like destroying the World Trade Center. Again, a broader perspective helps relieve the issue. We can use this event to make the world a better place. It already has. Do you remember feeling the global compassion on September 11? Wasn't it great when everyone involved put aside prejudices and exclusive belief systems to feel brotherhood and love? We noticed many acts of kindness and heroism as a result of that event. Many people learned more about themselves and what it felt like to be in that loving, caring state of consciousness. This is pure love.

That was its purpose. It is our choice whether we want to continue that feeling of compassion and love through forgiveness to heal the planet, or to play victim and blame games and destroy the planet.

As individuals we make our choices. Let's be courageous and authentic. Let's not buy into the old games of force and control. We do not, for any reason under the sun, have to be dominated or controlled in any way.

We have the power within to create peace in our hearts. If we express from our purified hearts, we can live peacefully with all those in our lives. We have the freedom to choose peace by being peaceful within ourselves.

We are realizing that our Life energy is directed outwardly to create our reality. We qualify and direct our energy through our thoughts and feelings. Life is not happening to us, we are creating it. We are now owning our own Divine authority and expressing ourselves naturally and authentically.

We are healing our hearts from past mis-creations with the energy of compassion and forgiveness. We are releasing programmed beliefs that create limitations in our minds. We are discovering how to use our creative abilities with a pure heart and pure imagination. With this new perspective we are now consciously creating our New World.

Destiny

Happy is the soul who attunes to the Divine
during the sacred journey of a lifetime.

Destiny is the target,
but the progress of evolution is the goal.

The Destiny of Every Man is Death

If you shall confront your Creator
at the time of death,

What then shall be your
purpose for living?

If you will be accountable
at the time of death,

Then by what standards
shall you live by?

If you can only save the
treasures of your soul,

Then what shall be regarded
as worthy investments?

If the destiny of every man
is death,

Then what has the pursuit of
happiness have in common
with life and death?

Happy Journey

We are a family of souls helping each other to reach our highest destiny.

Destiny is our aim in life. It's what we want to accomplish in terms of who we wish to become, what we want to experience, and what effect we want to have on others. From the higher-level perspective, we are evolving our souls. We are using life to refine who we are. We are purifying our expression of God's love. We are illuminating our virtues and talents along life's journey, shedding the remains of our ego like a chick emerging from its eggshell.

Our identity is shifting with our consciousness. Instead of thinking of ourselves as separate, we understand our qualities of uniqueness and our connection to All That Is. We are waking up to Oneness consciousness, the natural state of unity. We are the eternal essence of Spirit, knowing a greater part of Itself. We realize we are in natural communion with Nature.

If we tune in to our souls and learn what our own Divine plan is and stay tuned to Divinity, our road is not necessarily easy, but it's productive and fulfilling. Even when it feels difficult, we can still be happy. Deep inside we are fulfilling our life purpose by satisfying our soul's desires. Happiness comes from recognizing what desires are from our Higher Selves and serve the good of all, and what desires come from our egos that don't encompass love's wisdom and all-inclusiveness. We are choosing to come from love and be givers, rather than to satisfy selfish desires and be takers. As we focus on our goodness and let that expand, our love-light shines on our shadows. This enables us to release all pain while awareness emerges. We recognize God's blessings within the emancipated energy. Our shadows become our wisdom.

We sense wholeness and belonging when we fulfill the desires of our Higher Selves. We are being the love of God. As we become wise, we cherish every person, every mistake, every experience. We especially learn to accept and love ourselves more fully as God does.

The pursuit of happiness is such a fundamental desire from within each of us, its recognition was guaranteed by our founding fathers in the Constitution of the United States. They realized that to find our own happiness, we needed complete freedom to be and express. Freedom to speak our truth and make our own choices under Divine guidance grants us the peace and love that we so deeply desire.

Granting freedom to others to just be who they are, speak and be heard, exercise their own free will, and make their own choices, is paramount in these changing times.

Let go of expectations. Let go of jealousy. Let go of addictions. Let go of control and manipulation. Let go of greed or selfishness. Let go of fear. Surrender all of these aspects to God. They will be purified by the fire of love and returned as creative energy, wisdom, and love.

Choose happiness. Claim your freedom. Live peace. Express love. Be true to your Self. Value and honor who you are—realize your own Self-worth without need for external approval. Don't allow others to try to take away your free will. Do what you love to do. Be honest. Be authentic. Honor all of your feelings. Accept your human errors as part of the growth process. Don't condemn yourself or others. Forgive.

Have compassion for the process of life. We are all doing such a good job. For every person who vows to make choices of pure intent, based on love and goodwill toward all, many people become healed and whole.

There are no mistakes, only lessons. We choose love, or we gain a lesson in love. Now that we're waking up, we're learning a lot faster. Through our awakened awareness, we are assured that we are reaching our highest destiny, not only as individuals, but as a global family as well.

In our New World, we are choosing love.

Reality

Reality comes from our heart—It's called Love.

Love is Real

At first we understand what we see is what is real
The objects found within our life that we can touch and feel
Scientists prove what's real through physical observation
Leaving behind the reality of inner sensation

This subtle essence from which all things are made of
In its purity and stillness is God's presence sensed as love
This substance of reality is that which we all seek
Those that understand this are powerful, yet meek

People that know love as both substance and Source
Are no longer relying on competition or force
Our intentions form the essence of love moving through us
Creating who we are and all of our experience

Love is what is real and what satisfies our soul
Expressing it to our larger Self becomes our primary goal
Connecting to our Source, using it for alchemy
Creates for us dreams come true with infinite possibility

The Reality of Life

The prevalent notion of reality that is shifting consists of what we see and experience as physical form. If we can see and sense it with our five senses of sight, touch, hearing, taste, and smell, then we will confirm that it exists. As the saying goes, "Seeing is believing."

Now that we are waking up to how physical form comes into being, we will be using the opposite axiom in our new paradigm of reality: "Believing is seeing." We are becoming increasingly more aware that we are not only perceiving reality, but we are projecting it.

Quantum physics has helped us to make this giant leap. Peter Russell, in his book From Science to God, points out that consciousness and physical form have one thing in common—light. Sri Aurobindo further explains that: "all matter is just a mass of stable light."

The whole truth is that we not only perceive reality, but we create it within our consciousness. The way it works is that our thoughts direct the light of our consciousness. Light forms what we picture, or imagine, in our minds. It creates the structure.

The substance of form is energy. We are energy vessels. The energy that we are, in its most subtle form, is love. All of our emotions are one variety of love or another. Emotions are, essentially, energy in motion.

We create our reality, individually and collectively, with our thoughts and emotions.

Whether we are conscious of it or not, we create in every moment. Our thoughts, combined with our emotions, create physical form and experiences. The more attention, or direction of energy, we give to our thoughts, plus the intensity of our emotions, determines the solidity of the structure we create. The solidity means to what degree it manifests. It could be experienced as an event, or a life circumstance. It may become our experience, or another person may experience it. It may only pass through our dreams.

If we are not conscious, we may entertain our fears in our thoughts. We all know of the "what if" scenarios we've played out in our minds. Roosevelt said: "the only thing to fear is fear itself." The truth of that statement is that we are actually creating the reality, especially if we combine those thoughts with strong emotions. Now that we are aware, we are eliminating those negative thought patterns. We catch ourselves sooner and sooner and replace them with positive thoughts based on our conscious intentions. We learn to dwell on what we wish to create and experience.

When we begin consciously using Oneness awareness, we realize that "thoughts are in the air" as Einstein proclaimed, and that we can consciously choose which ideas to entertain. We send our life energy to the thoughts and ideas via our attention. Since we now realize we are creating in every moment, we dwell on and imagine what we would like to experience in our outer physical forms of reality. We are releasing our attachment to the mass consciousness and its programmed values and beliefs, and we are becoming free creators.

Eventually, we will always create from pure intent. Pure intent is driven by Divine will and pure love. Creative energy becomes married to inspired thought to create the manifestations of genius. This is the Holy Spirit of God doing through us.

The individual that experiences such Divine expression feels the ultimate joy that his or her soul is seeking. This type of experience is available to everyone. Indeed, it is the birthright of every soul, every child of God who walks this planet.

Perception

As we expand our perception of life to encompass God's view, or Total Awareness, the realization that perfections exists becomes evident in every moment of our lives.

Seasons of Life

For every time a season
For every life a reason
Evolving, changing, constantly
So much of it we do not see

Unconscious intention's energy
Forms into our reality
Creating experience to enjoy or endure
Soul intentions that are pure

Though often we don't understand
Peace is always close at hand
In some deeper sense we realize
All is perfect in God's eyes

An ever-present peace it brings
To sense perfection in all things
And even in what brings us pain
We're thankful for the blessings gained

Awareness will reduce our cries
As we open up our eyes
To see that every life has meaning
Incorporating truth we're gleaning

When perfection we cannot see
Our perception needs some deepening
At the highest level perfection exists
To realize this our search persists

A God's Eye View

When we are in the thick of our everyday lives, we are constantly making choices that affect our lives and the lives of those around us. A God's eye view is a higher perspective that helps us to make the highest choices with the most beneficial long-term effects.

When we have some resistance to another person or circumstance in our lives, a God's eye view helps us to move into the place where "what is" is accepted, understood, and appreciated. Our feeling of frustration disappears and we feel peaceful inside.

When we get irritated, the best thing to do is make a "perception adjustment." We look more deeply into the situation. With a higher-level perspective, we expand our awareness to include our whole life circumstances, how it affects our feelings, and what we might learn from the feeling of resistance. Sometimes we just have to note an awareness of "what is" and accept it. Then we can use that awareness to make intelligent choices.

All challenges have solutions. Our viewpoints may be clouded by past programming, perceptions distorted by negative thought patterns, beliefs that no longer hold true, or even just annoyances tainted by our moods. By rising above these personal viewpoints, we can find peaceful win-win resolutions.

How do we take a God's eye view? First of all, get yourself out of the way. Take out any self-interest based on perceived needs. These needs are the illusions of the ego: the need to be right, the need for approval, the need to be accepted, the need to feel superior or in control of situations or other people, or the need to express raw, unprocessed feelings such as anger. Ask yourself the question: "What is the perfect choice or solution that is for the highest good for all concerned?"

If you are having a challenge with someone you are relating to, take time out to process within your own being in quiet solitude. Look at the person objectively from a variety of perspectives. Most of all, try to see their perspective and understand them. Get into the life circumstances and the essence of the person. Take your feelings to God and express them fully. Ask for the wisdom within them to be revealed while feeling God's unconditional love.

When you have finished with your internal processing, communicate with the intention of mutual understanding and a win-win resolution. Ask them for their perspective and check out their reasoning. If they are open to it, pray together. Recognize the good in that person and express appreciation. This acknowledges the God in them and helps them to take a God's eye view, too.

Realize that we are all here, as souls, to evolve. Each person is doing the best they can in any given moment. Even people who are consciously trying to get better slip up. Forgive as quickly as you possibly can. It will help you both to move forward in peace.

When you find yourself in a situation that you find undesirable, first accept it. Look at the positive aspects and express gratitude. Sometimes the only thing positive is what you learned not to do again. Good. This is a great life lesson. Look at it long and hard so you don't repeat the mistake. Next, take a look at what choices lead you to this place in your life. Get the awareness out of it and move on. Get a clear idea of what your ideal situation would be.

When you become aware of energy that is undesirable or destructive to your life or being, move away from it. This is an act of Self-love. We can choose our proximity to people or situations, and love them or send positive healing energy from a distance. It's a great use of Oneness awareness.

With a God's eye view, we have the awareness of God's presence and availability to help with our perspective and possible solutions. We can set an intention to understand, and with that pure intent, understanding will come and feelings will shift back to peace. Peace in the now moment is always possible with a shift in perception.

We are not alone, ever. Help is always available. Pray for help or guidance. Talk to God and the angels. Miracles happen every day, and the more we ask for them, the more we experience them.

We can change or understand anything in our lives with the "perception adjustment" consciousness tool. This practice deepens our perception permanently in some ways.

In our New World, we are able to live with a lot more peace and ease with a higher perspective—A God's eye view— where everything is perfect "as is."

Paradox

By embracing paradox,
we claim our unity
and live in peace.

Paradox

We are all the same
We are each unique
Within the question   One circle is complete
Is the answer we seek   But spirals to infinity
                     When turned inside out   Outer form of experience
                     Exposing Divinity   Once called Reality
                                           In the land of relativity
                                           We notice duality

We observe polarity
Of opposite ends
We see black and white   Perception shift
Until rainbows bend   From outer flow in
                     Brings us to consciousness   Within we sense unity
                     Deep within   Looking out, our reflection
                                            Divinity expressed
                                            Brings love's perfection

Connecting, aligning
With the whole
Awareness of Oneness   Suddenly, expanded
And our own role   As each one integrated
                     Harmonious cooperation   Wisdom of all ages
                     Love's gift long awaited   Available to all
                                            Enfolded in feelings
                                            We hear our soul's call

Virtuous being
Illuminating light
In the joy of creating   Peace is here now
We shine so bright   And forevermore
                     We found the key   Paradox solved
                     We've opened the door   It's not this or that
                                            Love encompasses all
                                            That's where we're at

Unity Consciousness Applied

Unity consciousness holds that two seemingly opposing truths or ideas can exist simultaneously. For example, if one person expresses their truth, and another person expresses their truth about the same issue or circumstance with differing views, both can be right. This eliminates the need for argument and opens the space for acceptance.

Just as the six blind men who describe different parts of an elephant--one describing the trunk, the other the tusks, the other the skin, the other the tail, the other the feet, and still another the eyes—are all right from their perspective, so can we share our perspectives of life and all be right in describing our own truth.

The raw truth is in our feelings. We cannot argue with the "isness" of our feelings, nor can we invalidate the truth of the feelings of others. Communication of feelings within the energy of compassion deepens understanding with unity consciousness. The impact of our feelings on our personal experience often necessitates further communication, where interpretations vary based on individual filters.

Experience of life is garnered through our perspective and personal perceptions. Our perspective has to do with our relative location in the experience. We may actually see something different from our point of view, or where we stand in relationship to the experience or issue.

Our perception is sensing the experience through our scope of awareness—how narrowly or broadly we are seeing the issue or circumstance, and our filters of belief—what we hold as being possible in our mind. Our perceptions could be further colored by other mind stuff such as imagination or projection. This mind stuff may be adding additional energy that may or may not be true. However, if we are holding another's viewpoint in the space of acceptance, we can simply let it be. When we really try to understand it from their mindset, we broaden our own perspective.

With unity consciousness we stop focusing on either/or battles and create both/and solutions. We find it easier to compromise. Instead of having to compete to win or be right, we cooperate to set the stage for the next experience for win-win experiences. With love as our primary motivational force, we communicate with the intention to understand another perspective and we lose the need to be the only "right" perspective. This understanding expands our capacity to give and receive love.

In relationships of any kind, when unity consciousness is applied, we live in peace.

Just think of all of the possibilities for business when we engage in unity consciousness. Working cooperatively brings about new opportunities. People that are involved in the same type of business who share ideas and solutions spark greater creativity. They pool their resources and have more energy to focus on their unique applications.

In contrast to the energy of competition, these people don't have secrets or proprietary information. When people believe in themselves and their companies, they know that how they do what they do is special and unique. They know that there is enough business for all of them, so they don't have to live the illusion that there's not enough.

As governments apply unity consciousness, sharing and cooperation illuminates the diverse intrinsic worth of all cultures. This expansive openness shines the light of God upon all. Oppressive forces cannot exist in such light. The quality and richness of life expands beyond measure.

In our New World, unity consciousness breeds cooperation and peace.

Awareness

Ever-expanding
Awareness of Truth
opens us to Love.

Feeling in the Spaces

Space is an illusion
    For what we do not see
        But what we sense within it
            Is intelligent energy

It is consciousness that is present
    In that which is seen or not
        According to our expansiveness
            Thus we choose our lot

In any given moment
    Or in any scope of time
        Our expansion or contraction
            Of awareness serves our mind

The greater the expansion
    The more intensely we feel a bond
        This is the energy of love
            The power we ultimately count on

Space is rich with conscious energy
    Tapped by our imagination
        As we use the power of love
            We master our creation

As we co-create in a sea of love
    Celebrating our inventions
        We help and nurture each other
            The essence of love's intention

Know love saturates all spaces
    Let's bond in unity
        I feel the love in your space
            Can you feel the love in me?

Awareness of One Life

We are all One. The Life that flows through each one of us is connected and whole. We are part of that wholeness and we do exchange energies, although as an individual, we also have our own personal energy system. How do we really realize and experience our Oneness?

When we look outside ourselves, we see people, the earth, and objects. We see plants, minerals, and animals in and on the earth. When we look up into the sky, we see the sun and the clouds by day, the moon and the stars by night. The rest is space.

When we look at something under a microscope, we see finer details of what we are looking at. For example, when we observe a human cell, we see its various parts congealed by the fluid of the human body. When we further analyze the fluid, we see that it is made up of molecules that are further broken down into atoms. Between these subatomic particles there is space.

Space is everywhere, in everything. What is in the space?

Love and light are the energies in space, as well as in matter. It is also called Spirit. It is the essence of Life—the One Life that we all share. Any idea of separation is an illusion of perception. If we choose to experience Oneness as a known Reality, all we have to do is open our minds and hearts until they blend in pure consciousness.

Our mind is a tool, our laboratory, if you will. It's the place where we can receive or project ideas. It's also a place where we can contemplate, analyze, or synthesize. It does not always have to be on. When it is off or expanded by being still and quiet in perception mode, we tune in to consciousness. With this expanded awareness we can sense vibrations and sounds of love, and the colors and forms of light.

Our heart is the center of feelings. We can tune in to our hearts, feel the love that we are, and receive an abundance of love energy from God, our Source. To increase love, love more. Love God, love Self, love others. Love our planet, love animals, love plants, love earth. An open heart full of goodwill expands perception to increase awareness.

Love expands perception of awareness and awareness expands perception of love. Our mind can expand to perceive love, and our hearts can reveal the wisdom in feelings. It's a beautiful thing.

When we think of someone of whom we are bonded with love, they sense it. It is not an accident that when you often think of someone, they call. This is how Oneness awareness works. As we realize how to use Oneness awareness in this way, we will consciously increase our use of telepathy. Rather than call it a coincidence, we will understand how our energy expands and use it to contact people consciously.

Understanding is an expansion of awareness. As we expand our awareness to include the experiences and circumstances of others, we feel what they feel, and we understand them more fully. Communication of feelings and perspectives deepens our understanding and expands our awareness. The more people we understand, the more expansive our awareness, and the greater our capacity to love.

We can perceive personal and universal consciousness with the essence of our personal energy field. By expanding our awareness, we sense the fusion of our hearts and our minds. As we expand, we actually perceive the reality of Oneness.

The way to perceive spirit is through intuition. Intuition is the information we get from sensing the consciousness within us. No longer do we rely on our mind or our heart, but now we integrate the two for a full perception of Reality.

In our New World, we perceive Reality as being everything, seen or not. Space holds the very essence of Life. Sensing what is in space is the key to Oneness awareness.

Unity

United we stand, divided we fall.

You and Me—Polarity to Unity
—We are We

Precious moments in meditation
Extend joy to fruition and celebration
Inside we create the life we live
And manifest form with the love we give

Whether inner or outer experiences call
The truth is we are balancing all
In you I see what I might fear
You are my balancing angel, dear!

Your power and strength shines in your ray
Send some of that energy over my way!
My gentleness, love, and nurturing care
Is an abundance of energy that I will share

Intelligence, wisdom, voice of reason
Always in balance in its due season
Compassion, kindness from the heart
Flows through all and plays its part

Inwardly, outwardly we see our reflection
Divinity revealing its inherent perfection
Balancing aspects, becoming whole
Self mastering Life, realizing its goal

The yin and yang balances as life unfolds
The process itself reveals beauty to behold
Essence unraveling the veils of illusion
True Self awakens dissolving confusion

Versions of darkness and shadows emerge
Serving their purpose, Divinity's urge
It is Divine purpose that stands alone
Polishing, illuminating the light we're shown

Naught are pillars of you and me
But spirit entwined in a single tree
The tree of life both female and male
Melts into the child to tell its tale

The innocence of purity and open confession
Allows love's flow through truth's expression
Polar opposites as they attract
Gains for the other what each one lacked

Through attunement to God we realize perfection
As we begin to harmonize with our own reflection
Our gifts unfold as we integrate and balance
We illumine our virtues and discover our talents

No longer do we perceive a you and me
But the balancing act of Divinity
At once as Self is seen in all
We're open to receiving Heaven's call

We play our part in serving Humanity
Humbled, illusion no longer feeds vanity
Never more do we listen to ego's noise
We gracefully express with steadfast poise

Truly awakened into a Christed being
We see God's good in all that we're seeing
Of alpha and omega we derive our Source
Loving our God all along life's course

Becoming Whole

In our New World, we are becoming whole and becoming aware of being whole. First, we are becoming whole within ourselves. We are balancing our male and female energies. We have discovered our Inner Child. We are honoring our feelings for the wisdom they contain. We are being honest with ourselves. We are relying on our hearts to reveal truth to us with our heightened sense of intuition. We are using the power of love to illuminate our unique virtues. We love ourselves as we follow our heart's guidance.

Second, as we become Christed—living from our hearts in unity with our minds—we are sensing our connection to everyone and everything. We know we are truly connected and what we do with our energy affects others.

We begin the final stages of becoming whole within ourselves as we become motivated to seek and live truth. As we begin to turn our attention within and practice self-awareness, we start making choices for conscious self-improvement. At first we became egoically pleased to find that we could acquire and know an abundance of truth. However, like having food that is out of reach, it will not solve hunger. It's one thing to recite the truth and quite another to live it. We can feel truth, and we feel more alive with peace and joy when we are living it.

Now we see what we intend to be. We look inside our hearts and see what is truly good about us. We notice our unique virtues and talents and express them fully. We see where we have grown.

As we peel our layers of old energies by tuning in to our feelings, we understand what we resist in another is part of our own nature. Though we may deny and not express this quality, it is an energy that is emerging. The other person just acts as a mirror to show us our own reflection.

Sometimes, what we resist is a quality that we don't have. If someone irritates us because they seem to be coming on too strong, then that may indicate that we need to become stronger. Or, it may be the opposite where we need to become softer in some way. We may hang out with that person until we exchange energies to build up our own strength. That doesn't mean we express the energy in the same way, it is just a natural balancing mechanism of energy exchange.

Inside we are shifting from mental dominance to feeling dominance. We are receiving information directly through intuition. Our power comes from love. We no longer think of our mind as the seat of power, although we use it as a very powerful tool. Underneath thoughts are beliefs. Beliefs are what we hold to be true in our mind. We have been told what to believe in many cases, and we inherit belief systems. We are no longer available for the mental programming of beliefs.

While beliefs are mental positionalities that change, truth is absolute and eternal. We are now letting go of belief systems and we are learning the truth that we know inside our heart. "The truth is written in your heart." We can have faith in our own heart's perception of truth. We are tuned in to the truth—Universal Truth that cannot be twisted or distorted by human rationale, illusions of status, or positions of Old Paradigm power.

While we are peeling the layers of illusion and illuminating our own shadows, we are treating ourselves and others with compassion. For everything that exists, whether seen as dark or light, good or bad, has its purpose. When its purpose is finished, we part with it with gratitude for having served its purpose and bid it farewell. We transform the energy with love, back into love, and make something new. We make ourselves new. We actually renew ourselves as we recycle our personal energy to fit the form of our next ideal version of who we choose to be. We begin to use our personal Life energy consciously to create our experiences and circumstances in our life and in our world.

As we each look inside and find our guiding light, the Star of Bethlehem in our heart, we clearly see our union in God. We surrender to the Life that sustains us. We see the Good, the God, in all. We KNOW we are One.

Since we are reunited with our spiritual connection within, we know and sense our wholeness. We are beings of light. Our soulful essence is uniting and giving us a sense of strength and power within, as well as a sense of family and Unity without. We are Home.

It is Divine Purpose that stands alone as the hallmark of Unity. In our New World, we are experiencing the Ultimate demonstration of truth. As we stand united and strong, each living our own Divine Purpose, we are completing the dismantling of the old institutional structures of living. The new solutions that have emerged are based on heart-centered living within, and conscious cooperative living without. Within our hearts we are connected to the same Life force that is unfolding, expressing, and uniting through the loving intentions of Divine Purpose. We are connected to each other and we feel it.

Our United Life is an expression of Divine love. We are experiencing the grace of God. We are finding our way Home where Inner Peace abides, and we are creating Peace in our New World.

Purpose

Following our true heart's desire is our Life Purpose.
It strengthens our will to live and to give.
It is the vitality of Life expressing.

Finding Soul's Passion

Enthusiasm sparks when a heart is on fire
From the passion of the soul attaining its desire
As wisdom, creativity, and pure love are employed
Life feels joyful and the spirit is buoyed

Finding our passion as joy in our heart
Leads us to our mission, our individual part
As our purpose is discovered we claim inner peace
Fears, limitations, all blockages cease

The fire of love from our souls, who we are
We find it inside, it's not very far
By looking in deeply and often it's sure
Solutions are found, every pain can be cured

Checking in often to see what feels right
We're in tune with spirit all day and all night
With our spiritual connection we stay very clear
We know what we're up to and why we are here

We know we are love, meant to be expressed
Being kind to others makes us feel best
Deep inside we know we're all spiritual kin
Our compassion shared openly makes everyone win

We're all up to the same thing in a general sense
When we realize it's love we get off the fence
It's not time to wobble or waver right now
It's time to make a commitment, a spiritual vow

A simple vow to be ourselves, the best we can be
When we listen to our hearts it flows naturally
Openly and honestly communicating feelings
Opening up to sharing and healing

Feelings are the wisdom that our souls impart
Guiding us gently as they flow through our heart
Listening and following our soul's design
Fulfills our very essence for which we all pine

Let's turn up the love in our hearts and our life
Let's let love's fire burn away stress and strife
Let's create enthusiastically as we live our life's mission
Let's re-create the world now instead of just wishin'

Satisfaction

We inherently know that there is something greater than us that creates life and instills order in the Universe. This is Divinity. It is the purity of God. We were created in the image and likeness of God and have full access to our own individual Divinity. As we surrender to the power that runs the universe with complete faith and trust, we join in the flow of life. We get to know ourselves better and we believe in ourselves. We express who we truly are.

The order of the Universe is built around Purpose. When we find our own purpose and fulfill it, we satisfy our soul. We express our essential potential as illumined beings.

One day, in our own time, we come to realize that what we have been looking for all along is a deep sense of satisfaction—one that lasts. We get glimpses or flickers of it along our life's journey, like the time our child says something that really touches our heart, or like the time we reach out and help someone and they express how much they appreciate us. Sometimes we feel the elation of joy and enthusiasm sparked by the expression of our own unique creativity. Other times we may have expressed wise words that created an epiphany for someone. These are sobering moments when we can feel our very soul tingle with delight.

If we really stop to think about it, that feeling really does come from the depth of our souls. If we truly realize that these feelings really do come from our souls, then why not consciously try to satisfy our soul?

We are sparks of Divinity, waiting to be inflamed and expressed. Unique expressions of our own inherent virtues gain us the feeling that we are seeking. Although we have been swayed by propaganda towards unfulfilling values and experiences, the keenness of our souls discerns for us in our inner moments whether something serves us or not.

Universally, we are evolving into having goodwill toward all, or insuring that some form of love is our motivation for each choice we make. Our sense of Self expands along with our capacity to love. Individually, we are up to something more specific and personally oriented.

What can we inject in our everyday lives—right now in our present circumstances—to satisfy our souls? Where do we begin?

By reviewing your life to see what brings you joy, you can find and follow the path of your soul. You can discover what you are truly up to in this lifetime, your personal reason for living. You can create a personal life mission statement to articulate your clarity.

What are some of the highlights of your life? Look at when you created something that brought joy to your heart. You could look at actions that you took to help people (or plants, animals, or the environment) and what the nature of those actions were. You can check out the positive patterns in your life. What do those patterns suggest in terms of your values, your personal impact in the world, and your favorite form of creative expression?

What is your highest value? Honesty, freedom, integrity? Search your heart until you find it. Review your conversations. What have you stood for in the past with passion?

Who are you concerned the most about? Your Self, children, animals, the environment? What issue do you feel really strongly about? What kind of action have you taken or who have you teamed up with on this issue? Is there something you've been meaning to do, but haven't taken the next step? As you gain clarity and take life one step at a time, life falls into place.

How do you like to express your creativity? Do you build, paint, make crafts, sing, or write? Remember some incident of feeling tremendous joy from something you made or did that was creative. Wouldn't you like to do more of that?

Try combining what kind of impact you want to have with your life, who you would like to impact with your life, your highest value and your favorite form of expression into one short statement. For example, "My mission is to inspire (impact on others) children (who) to live their truth (highest value) through my writing (favorite form of expression)." This is your life mission. Play with it until it feels good. You'll know when you get it right—it will feel like it fits, just like when you find clothes or shoes that fit just right and you feel comfortable and proud. Feel your soul smile!

By looking at your light within and gaining clarity about your life's purpose, you will surely be highly motivated and enthused to carry on with your soul's intentions. We get inspired every time we give our soul such attention! If this becomes a regular practice, the fires of passion will inflame your heart and the brightness of your soul's joy will light the way to your highest destiny.

What a wonderful way to experience lasting satisfaction! We are using our unique creative expressions joyfully to make positive contributions in our New World.

Expression

As we open to Divinity's expression,
we call our unique potential to fruition.

Life Expressing

Candle flame
Emitting light
Bursting atoms
Implosive energy

Cosmic thought
Universal field
Human reception
Perceptive process

Outside in
Inside out
Passion flows
Life expressing

Prana feeds
Chi current
Soul voice
World emergence

Conscious Intelligence
Human reception
Image kaleidoscope
Unique creation

Intelligent energy
Cosmic force
Flowing freely
Life expressing

Personal Divinity

At our very core of essential Self lies Divinity, Life Itself, waiting to be expressed. When we place our attention inside, in our hearts, we open Heaven's Gate and begin to know and express our True Selves. Pure love, wisdom, and joy come from this place.

In our home of hearts, we find infinite wisdom to be called upon. Just sitting still in silence offers us the opportunity to tap into the riches of the universe and our own Divine potential. We can ask the universe any question at any time. Many times we get direct answers, other times we get them through some person, media, or experience in life. As we practice with silence and meditation, we become more and more proficient of receiving detailed direct answers.

Our true nature is Universal love that is unconditional. It's what we grow into as we expand our capacity to love through our expanding awareness and loving expressions. It takes practice. We're growing out of old paradigm rules and beliefs about relationships now. Our range of choices aren't so narrow. In fact, we are free to love as we express our truth of being through our feelings.

We are learning to accept and understand each other. When we know our true selves, we don't have to accept or personalize the judgments of others. Thank goodness we are learning not to judge each other. Now let's try to go easier on ourselves, too. One of the hardest things we're up against is accepting and loving ourselves, even when we make mistakes. We are often hard on ourselves because we have the natural propensity to evolve. However, part of this evolutionary process is to learn to love ourselves unconditionally, just as we are right now. This unconditional self-love is foundational. The more we take conscious, active steps to love ourselves, the more we can grow into loving others. What are you doing to love yourself today? Could you ask yourself that question every day?

We become more and more aware of our ideals and aspirations as we look into our true unique nature. Just by holding the vision of who we choose to be and where we are going in the same now moment as being unconditionally accepting and loving of ourselves, we plant the seeds of our own creation of life. Nature takes us there, magically, once we set loving intentions.

While being in silence, we can find our life's purpose just by simply asking the question: "Why am I here?" Listen to hear the response of your inner voice. The more it is asked and as time goes on, the more detailed answers we receive. When we are clear about what we are up to in life and go about the business of fulfilling our personal life purpose, we are expressing our personal Divinity. This brings our souls great joy, and boy, do we feel it!! As we stay tuned to God through meditation, intuition, and by following the joy in our hearts, we stay on our course and make necessary adjustments as we go along.

Constant evaluation and adjustment is needed to flow with life's changes. We are operating as part of a whole. We take into consideration life's data of:

"what is" in each moment, our feelings, choices made by others that affect our decisions, spontaneous events and circumstances, the synchronistic flow of connections and opportunities, and Divine guidance.

In this New World, I am happy to announce, we are all much brighter and joyful as we express ever-deeper love, fascinating wisdom, and incredible creativity. Our experiences of each other as we each express our unique personal Divinity is making our lives richer and more deeply satisfying.

Honesty

Simply being honest helps us to experience life more fully.

Susan Campbell
Getting Real

Authenticity

I'll tell you from my heart how I feel
As I express who I am today
But tomorrow I may change
And feel another way

I speak and live my truth
And I express in my own fashion
Please try to understand me
As I reveal my inner passion

I'm just living along in life
Doing the best I can
I have my share of challenges
I hope you understand

Each of us has our point of view
And we can both be right
Let's compromise for peaceful solutions
So we don't have to fight

Sometimes I laugh at myself
When I catch my own mistakes
But if you judge or ridicule me
I cry as my heart breaks

And if you shout in anger
That pierces my very soul
The damage runs so deep
It's difficult to console

I hope you really listen to me
Is it compassion that you feel?
Because I am being authentic here
Being really real

I love your appreciation
For things I make or do
I love it when you laugh at me
It's fun to be silly, too

I'm just being myself
As weird as that may seem
Although we may be different
We are still on the same team

Showing Up for Life

Being real is showing up for life with complete honesty around our feelings. As we really tune in to our feelings, and consider the feelings of others, we transform our very being. We access our inner knowingness of truth.

Welcome to our New World where people care about how they show up for Life. So many beautiful, loving souls have emerged. They are shining their light so bright; the darkness of illusion just can't exist!!

The illumined souls who have shed their egos and surrendered to Life, to God, have lit the way for us to live the truth. This is our gift back to Life—our service to the world. Our accelerated evolution has paved the way for positive, drastic, and sometimes instantaneous, change. Miracles are occurring all around us right now.

The simple key to being real is "Just be your Self." How can anything be more simple? All we have to do is show up for life and get real. First, we have to get honest with ourselves. We find out what is real and pure about ourselves. We check in with our feelings. We ask ourselves: "What layers of defense reactions can I now notice and release?" What feelings have been repressed that are now coming up for processing. By paying attention to our true feelings, we sort ourselves out.

When we shed our egoic layers, we reach the core of who we truly are. We find ourselves, and in so doing, find God. The spark of Divinity that is in each one of us always finds expression. There's nothing that we need to be that we aren't already. As soon as we really know, understand, and love ourselves unconditionally, we naturally begin to know, understand, and love others.

With compassion we can treat our feelings as our child. A child who needs to feel cared about and nurtured. We tend our Inner Child by honoring, understanding, and communicating our feelings. We sit with them with total acceptance and compassion and hear their wisdom in silence. We heed them by applying their wisdom in our lives.

Caring about feelings is caring about God. Consider in the Bible when Jesus was talking about denying Him three times. Remember how God said to come to Him as a child? What do you think Christ Consciousness is? When we explore our feelings with the innocence of a Child, we come to know God. When we deny our feelings, we deny God by denying our True Self.

We naturally become compassionate when we tune in to our feelings. We understand that others have the same life challenges and range of feelings that we have. With our compassionate nature, we become very kind and gentle creatures. Our inner senses have become heightened and we sense God in nature and in everyone.

49

As we consciously evolve, we become more and more attuned to the feelings of others. We really care how they feel. We care how our words and actions affect them. Being conscientious of the feelings of others causes us to be kind, considerate, and compassionate.

Showing up in life means being concerned for Life itself. Showing up as an expression of love is the ultimate goal of the consciously evolving soul. It is caring.

In our New World we truly care about one another. We help. We forgive easily. We abstain from judgment. We accept others for who they are. We don't try to exert our will over others. We don't manipulate or control for self-serving purposes. We love who we choose to love, and we let others love who they choose to love, without judgment, jealousy, or expectation.

Not only do we express ourselves in this way to others, but we extend the same level of kindness to ourselves. We forgive ourselves for mistakes or shortcomings. When we become aware of them, we set in motion the process of change through our intention. We don't judge ourselves. We claim our free will and guard it within our hearts and minds. We are aware of our feelings and allow them to guide us to our truth.

We speak our truth with compassion. Open honesty is honoring love. Even if the truth is not well received, we don't react to reactions. We allow the expression of others.

We communicate with the intention to understand, both when we speak and when we listen. It is our soul's deepest desire to be understood. By reflecting our understanding of others, they feel fulfilled. No longer do we need to defend a position to be right. We just long to be heard and understood. With the common ground of understanding, we can move forward into new levels of love, wisdom, and creativity.

Listening with our hearts to each other, being very present energetically without any opinion or positionality, and understanding the essence of the message from the soul, is the best gift of all and the easiest to give. In this energy, we feel free, we feel grateful, we feel pure love.

We are now, more than ever, open, honest, and real. Our sense of love is deepening and raising the quality of life. We are showing up as our authentic self. Thank God we are listening to, and really hearing, ourselves and others in our New World.

Integrity

In our minds we see possibilities,
in our hearts we know truth.

Integrity is speaking and living the truth
that we know in our hearts.

Living Truth

Knowing Self
From inner core
Truth is found
Through heaven's door

Honesty of feelings
No right or wrong
Uniquely expressing
One's own song

Free will to make
Individual choice
Unhampered makes
A soul rejoice

Expressing love's wisdom
Living truth
Innocent and humble
Renewable youth

Responsibility for
Impact on others
Respecting all
Sisters and brothers

Integrity of being
Compassionate, kind
In God's pure reflection
Our virtues we find

Impeccable truth
In every word
Expression of love
Always insured

Cosmic Law

Cosmic Law, also known as Universal Law, is embedded in the very energy of Life. It holds us responsible and accountable for how we spend our Life Energy. Cosmic law is the law of love and balance. Love lights up the truth revealed in our feelings, and as we speak and live our truth, we stand in our own integrity. We are living according to Cosmic Law when we come from a place of love and have goodwill toward all. The Universe provides a balancing mechanism to teach us when we don't come from love and goodwill.

The laws of energy, specifically the laws of thermodynamics, magnetics, and electricity provide us with the information we need to utilize our energy at our fullest capacity with the most efficient and beneficial results. The details of how to understand and use Life energy is revealed in my upcoming book: Live Love : How to Help Create A Better World Now. The application of this understanding enables us to express our full Divine potential. For now, a basic understanding of balance will suffice.

When we honor and love all of our feelings within, wisdom emerges. Acting from this wisdom keeps us in integrity. We are calibrated by attuning to our soul through our heart, part to whole, soul to Spirit, and live in balance and harmony with all of Life.

We qualify our life energy with our thoughts and feelings and then act accordingly. Whether we send out our qualified energy positively or negatively, the same energy is cycled back to us multiplied. In our New World, the law of balance is swift.

We have free will to use our personal life energy constructively or destructively. Since life energy in its purest form is love, consistent love motivation and generation is our goal. We aspire to use our energy as purely as possible. We consider our impact on others.

In our New World, we have an expanded awareness of Self. We know we are One. Living the truth of our Oneness causes us to display goodwill toward all. We put Jesus' words "Do unto others as you would have them do unto you" into action not as an act of obedience, but because we truly understand that everyone is part of our larger Self. It benefits us on an energetic level to benefit others.

We are conscientious about our behavior, how we treat ourselves and others. For all energy expressed through our behavioral choices, we eventually experience what it feels like to be on the other side. Sometimes grace may be bestowed upon us to lighten our karmic loads, but we are here having a human experience so that we can become purely Divine and live the truth of love. Integrity is living and expressing our truth.

Cosmic Law does not permit us to tamper with another's free will choices. We do not have the right to control another person. We do not have the right to use oppression or force in any way. If we choose to positively affect another, we can act as a model of love or "love the hell right out of them." The energy of love expressed always produces positive results.

As individuated aspects of God, we are unique souls. We each have an individual mission for our life. We each have unique individual qualities. It is up to us to truly know our True Selves. When we are still and silent and look within, we find our own truth. Our feelings and desires reveal our pure God essence. By experiencing our feelings internally with awareness, we really come to know ourselves.

We access our Mother-God aspect when we place our attention deep within our hearts. We feel the God-love that we are. We find our joy and follow it. We are discovering all of the goodness within ourselves and expressing it. We are increasingly communicating our feelings with compassion. All feelings, even fear and anger, when processed internally with compassion, can be transformed back into love. The truth within them, such as personal boundaries or choices, can be spoken with kindness. We are honoring ourselves. We are being true to ourselves as a top priority. That's integrity.

By uniting with Father-God, or Universal Mind, we are finding unlimited ideas and inspiration flowing through us. We know all wisdom comes from God and we don't puff ourselves up. We know we all have equal access to our Universal Mind. We are humble. That's integrity.

As we become pure of heart by releasing all past pains with love and forgiveness, we blend our intelligence with love. Our heart and mind become one and our Inner Child is born. We experience our vulnerability and ask for help with the innocence of a child. As we open to our Inner Child, pure creativity flows. We know that all life energy comes from God and we share our gifts openly and generously. That's integrity.

Each person and circumstance in our life was chosen by us. Although we may resist a particular person, that person was invited into our lives by our Higher Self for a reason. Even when a person or circumstance doesn't seem beneficial to us, they always are. If we accept the gift of the opportunity to grow through all relationships and circumstances while remaining in integrity, we evolve our souls. We accomplish the higher-level goals that we set for ourselves when we designed this life experience.

By standing in our own integrity, we are changing the world to a place of love and freedom. Our New World is once again an age of Golden Opportunity.

Forgiveness

Forgiveness becomes appreciation
when we truly understand Life.

Being Human

If we can be honest in that we are human,
cannot we be honest in every other
aspect of our lives?

And is it not human to err?

Aren't the virtues of the soul
ever- present?

Then why not tune in to our souls
and draw upon those virtues?

And forgive ourselves and others
for our humanness.

And <u>love</u>.

Healing Feelings with Forgiveness and Compassion

Human nature meets our Divine essence and provides opportunity to experience life for the sake of evolution. The old saying that "to err is human and to forgive is Divine" holds a truth that reveals compassion for the nature of Life. Our Divine essence seeks to express purely in its melding with the human nature. Our essence holds the potential of expressing cosmic consciousness, while human consciousness blends the biological, environmental, and cultural filters in our thoughts and feelings. Each have elements that influence our actions with seemingly separate wills.

Until the wills of both the Divine and human qualities are unified in consciousness, there is conflict and challenge. Until there is integration and balance of body, mind, and soul through the heart, feelings of discord and confusion result.

Ultimately, the person most difficult to forgive is our self. We may have set personal goals and not attained them immediately, if at all. There have been times when we have hurt the people we love. Sometimes we have undermined our own accomplishments with inharmonious behavior. At times we have damaged our own health through negative thoughts, feelings, or behavior patterns. When awareness of what is true for and about us is not in alignment with our expression, our natural propensity to evolve is active. The process itself is perfect. We can relax into the knowing that we are evolving naturally. There is no reason to judge or criticize ourselves for this evolutionary drive. Life is a process, and Divine Mercy shows us how to compassionately forgive ourselves and to love unconditionally.

When we feel damaged or betrayed by others, it is imperative that we forgive to heal our own inner and outer worlds. As we heal our feelings with forgiveness, we release heavy energy and feel lighter. When our inner pain is lit up by another's actions, often we initially blame the other person for our feelings. When we take a deeper look, we find our own relationship patterns have revolved around our soul's attempt to resolve core issues within us. It is the healing and release of these core issues that are our tickets to our New World of Peace. As we heal our old wounds, we are releasing our shadows, illuminating our light, and shining bright.

Eventually, we realize the blessing in our experience with the person we initially blamed as well as the resulting feelings. All of our feelings contain wisdom. When we apply a conscious process of healing with forgiveness, all that remains in the end is appreciation of the experience, appreciation of the person who played their part in the experience, and the wisdom that becomes a part of who we are. We take responsibility for co-creating these painful experiences, and we know they are blessings to our soul.

The process of healing feelings begins with treating our inner selves with compassion for having endured the experience. Then we look at other times we have felt the same way all the way back into our childhood, and possibly even beyond, into our past lives. When we get to the root of this issue, we can then consciously release our defense mechanisms that block our flow of energy. By loving our feelings with compassion and understanding their roots, we elicit their wisdom and transform the energy consciously back into love.

Love heals at the very deepest levels. Compassion is the key. As we apply these high vibrational energies to ourselves, we become more of these qualities. Then we have more to give others. The so-called dark aspects of ourselves are actually great gifts of potential just waiting to be expanded into wisdom through the energy of love. As we reach our core and transform this potential into expression, we are free to be who we truly are—the Light of Love.

Once we have resolved our own core issues, we can communicate our feelings within our relationships with compassion. We can draw our boundaries with firm resolve. We don't have to allow ourselves to be mistreated, but when we draw experiences into our lives, we must first do our inner homework, then we can say "no" to circumstances, events, or relationships.

When others know they have wronged us with destructive energy, it is most beneficial to forgive them immediately. However, forgiveness may be a process that is handled in steps over time. When we need space to process and heal, we can communicate that in a kind way and take the time and space we need. As we process, we can love all energies (our feelings, their feelings) as our own and apply unconditional love within to them and to ourselves. The bonding that occurs fulfills the deepest desires of our heart and soul. Wisdom emerges. The sense of connection strengthens. This is true conscious soul evolution.

In our New World, we are peeling away layers of past pain residue, past unconscious mis-creations, and we express the Divine love, wisdom, and power that we are. We are shining brightly, and our Earth is becoming a star!

Transformation

As we congeal spirit with matter, our souls with our bodies,
and our minds with our hearts, we bring Heaven to Earth.

Our inner dormant senses are awakened and we are
reborn into another dimension of consciousness.

Love transforms.

Waking Up In Transformation

O'er land and sea did they travel
Mysteries of life to unravel
Observed the human nature change
Mind, body, soul rearranged
Waking up in transformation
Still sleepy; not out of incubation
Wonders of new life form now
Feelings, senses, changed somehow
Smacks of Oneness in spirituality
Confirmed by science in reality
Awareness shift from man's outward leap
Conscious now; going in deep
Emerging senses of peace and love
Different perspective below and above
Waking up in transformation
Dormant senses experience elation
Body acquiring ever more chi
Yoga balancing new energy
Words emanating from mind to yield
Increasing reception from unified field
Stillness, quiet, meditation
Forever altering man's vibration
Hearts absorbing cosmic love
Oneness threads so spoken of
Woven through all aspects of being
Man is now conclusively seeing
No longer to be hypnotized
Soul connection realized
Waking up in transformation
Sending out more invitations
Conscious intentions; goodwill to all
Expanding awareness; inner call
Constant practice of meditation
Heightening, expanding, new revelation
Inner wisdom surfaces as intuition
Dreams come true as its fruition
Enlightenment consciousness begins to exist
Lower thought forms no longer persist
Changing, transforming those who partake
Conscious beings do they make
Pillars of light and energy
Creating a new reality

The Paradigm Shift

Awareness of the Paradigm Shift varies according to the receptivity in each of our hearts and minds. Some may not even have identified it as such, others may be acutely aware of the inner and outer transformation taking place. However, we all have learned different aspects of it and have had our own unique experiences. For the purpose of summarizing and creating a common understanding, I'm going to share an overview of this global evolutionary shift from my perspective.

The Paradigm Shift is a global, as well as individual, "awakening" process. We have been birthing a new level of consciousness. We are changing who we "thought" we were to who we really are as souls and coming to more fully express our Divinity. As Children of God, we are becoming aware of our abilities, virtues, powers, and responsibility. We have been learning to receive Life Energy, from God, our Source, directly and consistently by placing loving attention in our hearts with gratitude.

We are realizing our ability and power as creators, and we are learning to co-create our personal and global reality with God according to the Divine Plan. As we each discover the purpose for our individual lives, we are following our passions to become better "beings" and create a better, cleaner, harmonious world. We are creating, each with our unique expressions, a world of beauty and peace with the Love that we essentially are.

In the process of becoming Conscious Creators, we are recognizing that we have been trapped in outdated belief systems that do not serve us. Now we know we can choose what to believe, and to listen to the God Truth in our hearts. The more we listen and pay careful attention to our feelings, the more our senses of intuition and telepathy increase. We are using our awareness of Oneness. Our "cause and effect" world has quickened and synchronicities abound. We are realizing the causal aspects of our nature. We are noticing the effects by claiming responsibility for the state of our lives, and the state of the world. Our heightened clairsentience, the inner knowing of Truth, is having a profound impact in our lives and world affairs.

As we live for Truth, we don't need any mental or emotional filters to distort our perceptions or creations. We are removing these "blockages" through Self-imposed purification processes in the form of difficult relationships or experiences. The whole world is being purified by certain events and positive energy focus.

We are coming to accept and express our feelings and release past patterns of denial and repression. Now we have new processes to deal with our feelings. As we employ them, we are discovering the wisdom in our feelings—the wisdom from God. The most fascinating thing is that we have stored all these feelings and "core issues" from past life patterns as well, and as we resolve them we are obtaining the blessings of "Revelations!" These are insights about Life, ourselves, and our Divinity.   These are solutions to personal, community, or world challenges. These are glimpses of God's Vision for our New World and our part in it!

We are realizing how good we really are. We know our own Divinity and no longer do we accept criticism of unkindness into our lives because we know our true inherent value and have the highest concepts of self-worth. We love our Freedom to express our True Selves, cooperate with others, and create in a state of joy. We are coming to love all unconditionally, starting with ourselves. With the energy of compassion we are healing ourselves, each other, and the world.

We are realizing that Life is eternal. With that awareness, we have no fear of death. The loss of our loved ones is tempered with the knowledge that we can still communicate with them now, and that we will reunite with them within a common realm one day.

We are all learning to focus our attention on the energy of love in its myriad forms, and to "turn the other cheek," or face our attention away from that which we no longer choose to experience or have exist. We focus our attention with love on what we consciously choose to create with goodwill toward all. Everybody is winning now.

The fire in our hearts is blazing! We have more passion that we channel into our ever-deepening relationships and our life missions. As we serve our world with a sense of cooperation and Brotherhood, we are each having a tremendous impact. We don't feel helpless or hopeless any longer. We are love in action!

We are Home in our Hearts and we know we are all united as One in the Spirit of God. We are aware of our unified consciousness now. We know we can't help but have an effect on one another, so we are kind, considerate, and responsible.

We are awake and more alive than ever before!!

With the inherent Freedom that rests in our minds, we are creating a New World, after all.

Essence

Essence is the subtle energy of Spirit,
eager to share its wisdom and love.

Ego Transformation

Our ego is the container that we call "I"
It's a focal point of consciousness, one of God's eyes
While we are programmable and under illusion
We believe we are separate, not sensing our fusion

Although we are one loving intelligent spirit
Some guard their egos, others may fear it
But as we awaken directing attention to our core
We realize our essence and seek for more

The container of our ego opens up like a sieve
Feeling and expressing love, really learning to live
Oneness awareness causes consideration of our impact on others
Developing a deep sense of family, all sisters and brothers

Our fear is abated as we retain our individuality
We help humanity heal all forms of brutality
Our uniqueness increases as we express our essence
The gift of who we are offers many presents

As we trace the rays of our essence to God, our Source
We navigate with love along life's course
Suddenly we begin evolving at lightning speed
We realize unlimited Source, absolving all greed

As we learn to share openly our own perspective
We open to others, too, as a primary objective
Each of us has awareness of one little part
And our awareness expands as we open our heart

At our mutual core of Source we're all the same
With compassion we can help each other in life's loving game
As we express from our essence life joyfully unfolds
We appreciate God and all life as beauty to behold

Dedicated to God, the love of my life and the life I love!

Communicating as Aspects of God

As our awareness expands, I notice we tend to use the same terminology and we don't necessarily communicate our true perspective.

For example, the word "I" is used in so many connotations, it sometimes get confusing. It is not just a pointer to the egoic self, but it denotes an individual entity of existence, or where the focal point of consciousness is placed. Each individual entity is a focal point of consciousness that expands and contracts. The nature of life and of consciousness is to expand and contract.

As we are awakening, our very concept of self-identification is shifting, expanding.

God is All That Is. There is only one consciousness in the All That Is. From God do all things and people come, but it would not serve communication to call everything and everyone God. So when we refer to ourselves, we say "I" and we have names for all other aspects of God as well. It is a place of observation that gives us our individual perspective. We are not the identity of where we are, which is always changing. Our "I," or observing eye, can be directed consciously to place attention on that which we wish to create as our Self and our experience. Our egoic casing is a sense of identity that is simply who we "think" we are. It is an illusion of mis-identification with aspects of our lives that differentiate and separate us from others, and even from our True Self. The reference to "I" is now changing its meaning as we are shifting in consciousness.

The awakened soul, although aware of our inherent Oneness, still uses these terms, but our perception, which is not always communicated or understood, is grounded in the knowledge of our wholeness.

Sometimes the ego gets a bad rap, but it certainly has its purpose. It serves as a container in which we can define ourselves as individuations of the one Spirit in which we are an aspect. It's like an eggshell, a container, in which we develop self-identity. When we begin to become aware of our True Self, our unique essence, the eggshell casing of the ego breaks down so that our unique essence can shine.

To identify with the ego as our whole self is to be unconscious of our unique Essence and Oneness with Spirit. It is a case of mistaken identity. We are identifying with a mental construct, or "image" of who we are, rather than the truth of who we are. That is when we think we are this life, this body, this job title, this cultural being, this gender, this race, this economic state, this feeling, this action, or this thought. As long as we are fully aware of our Oneness, we can let go of our ego. As Self-realized beings, we know that we are aspects of God, individuations of the one whole Spirit.

As our soul evolves naturally through the experience of life, we discover the truth of our inner nature. We are Divinity in expression. Natural evolution is a process of discovering and embodying the truth of our essential being. We express the virtues of the soul in our outer expressions. Our truth is contained in our cellular structure. It is not only who we are, but what we are. This embodiment of our truth comes most easily when we step out of the way of ego identification and express our true nature, spirit.

We discover our truth from our cellular being inside, and then express it fully and creatively, leaving behind all programmed patterns pertaining to the unconscious notion of being a separate self. Our expressions become God-like as we show up more and more purely as our unique expressions of unconditional love, beauty, wisdom, creativity, and compassion, or whatever aspect of the divine that we choose.

Even as we express our true nature, we refer to our personal experience, or our focal point of consciousness, as "I." However, as we become more natural and express pure spiritual energy, we also become more attuned to energy. Tuning in to this energy facilitates communication. Have you ever had the experience of someone slipping and saying the wrong word, and you didn't even notice because you understood the essence of their communication?

Communication at the level of feeling develops in the awakened individual when we sense energy. Sometimes it creates clear understanding, and other times it creates confusion when the verbal communication doesn't match the energy we're sensing. That's a signal to check for integrity. Trust the feeling and get the truth from that. Express the truth of the feeling, and more will be revealed.

As we awaken to our Oneness and realize that everything and everyone is an aspect of God, we can also be aware of the change in communication. At first there may be some dissonance because words are relied on too heavily, but as we communicate and express what we feel, our communication is becoming cleaner and the genuine meaning or understanding of "what is" is surfacing. With our inner senses attuned, there is no confusion between the egoic "I" and the "I" who is the individuation of divine essence. We feel each other's essence now.

We are sensing beyond words for communication, and the truth that we feel is paramount. It is deepening our experience of love. In our New World, our hearts and souls are fulfilled and we are elated!

Light

Life is light is love.

Shine So Bright

Inner light
Shine so bright
Everything is clear
There really is no darkness
There is no need to fear

With so much love
I have for me
Inside is where I live
When I go out
I have courage
I have a lot to give

Inner light
Shine so bright
My Inner Child is healed
Lifting layers of pain
That used to be my shield

With so much love
I have for God
And that God has for me
I always feel peace deeply
No matter what I see

Inner light
Shine so bright
Radiate love that soothes
Touch the souls in my life
With my every move

With so much love
For humankind
And everything on Earth
Inspiring love to wake in all
Realizing their great worth

Illuminating the Virtues of our Soul

We are beings of light—lovelight. As we express our True Selves, we shine so bright.

When our unique virtues are expressed, boy we can really feel it! What bliss! We are illuminated. We have that great feeling inside—soul pride—and the exuberant joy of unique expression makes us feel special. We are special! Each of us is so-o-o-o special, just like a snowflake.

We each have special talents, skills, and abilities. We have special characteristics and personal qualities. We have special interests and passions. And, we have our own special way of expressing ourselves.

Our feelings of passion are the fire of Spirit igniting our soul. That is how we recognize all of our unique virtues. Our life's direction, guided by our strongest passions, allows Divinity to spring forth. It is the essence of Life expressing.

The essence of our soul is pure, too. In our New World, we have discovered that with the shedding of the ego, we are also releasing "what we think we are." We're letting go of old thought patterns that no longer serve our highest good and beliefs that were handed down to us. With this letting go, we are free to express the essence of our souls.

Take a look at your life. What makes you feel really good about yourself? Is it how you treat others? Are you helpful, nurturing? Do you make a good friend, being there when someone needs you? Do you have a hobby that brings you great joy?

What are your talents? Are you good at building? Do you express your creativity through art, writing, or music? Are you a great problem-solver? Do you help people through your healing abilities? Are you good at creating a warm and esthetically pleasing home space? Are you good at business, negotiating deals, or knowing what the customer wants?

What are you passionate about? Is your concern for the environment your primary motivating force? Do you feel strongly about how governmental bodies should function and how the people within this institution should behave as representatives of the people? Are you passionate about justice or freedom? What solutions for our world do you see?

What are you interested in learning more about? Is it self-improvement, such as exercise or taking better care of your health? Is it figuring out how something works? Is there some new skill you would like to acquire?

What are your most admirable characteristics? Are you kind or helpful? Are you generous? Are you a good listener? Are you accepting and understanding of yourself and others? Are you honest? Are you responsible? Are you intuitive? Feel your Self glisten as you take note of your true being.

Light up your passion. Whatever brings you the most enthusiasm within yourself illuminates your virtues. Dwell on these personal talents and qualities often. You may wish to create a list of your best qualities and talents and review them daily. Remind yourself of what you are passionate about, or what form of creative expression brings you joy. Feel your self-love expand. Notice how your inspiration increases. Notice how your self-worth becomes stronger. Be open to bringing your inspired ideas into physical reality by taking action steps.

Honor your Self. Your essence, expressed from the inside out, allows the flow of Divinity and brings an ever-increasing feeling of vitality.

Love your Self by illuminating your virtues. As you shine the light of awareness upon your virtues, anything that is false about who you thought you were will dissipate and disappear in the light of Who You Truly Are. Your True Self shines.

Shine on, unique soul!! We need you in our New World.

Reflection

When we interface with Life as our own reflection,
we unify our own aspects of self within and
come into balance and wholeness.

Reflecting Your Light

It is my deepest pleasure as you run your energy through my soul
To reflect your light right back to you and help you reach your goal
Of mastering your self and creating who you choose to be
Letting nature unfold naturally

The mirror that I am, the things you love in me
Are all about yourself my friend, those are the things you see
And if you don't see my qualities, my strength I hold inside
Then you don't see yourself— hey, you don't have to hide

And you know your dark side that you have now revealed?
That's just like me and you know it, my layers have been peeled
Together we exchange energies and we mutually evolve
As we experience our Oneness and meet our soul's resolve

I am not the only one that comes into your space
How much do others reflect you, can you see it in their face?
As we sense each other's energy field, consciously exchanging
We realize we are shifting this world, beneficially rearranging

So conscious are we all of our current transformation
We bond our visions powerfully for a heavenly creation
Where the rivers of love run deep through our souls
And we treat each other as precious as gold

The Opportunity of Reflection Awareness

Realizing that we magnetize the quality of energy that we put out through our feelings, thoughts, words, and actions, we know that what and who we draw into our lives to create our experiences are reflections of ourselves.

This seems to be a very "rude awakening" when we draw people or circumstances into our lives that seem irritating and destructive, causing us misery. However, it is just part of the awakening process. Whenever we decide to build something new, the old needs to be taken down and transformed. Since everything in life is energy, the energy of our old selves is brought to the surface to be transformed into our new selves.

The happy side of this coin is that what we admire in others is also a reflection of ourselves. We are graduating into Self-love and a sense of high personal value as we weed out our old patterns and subconscious beliefs about ourselves by using our relationships to consciously evolve.

Our self-awareness practice of going within—to reflect on how we see our own traits show up in others—provides us the opportunity to feel what resonates with who we are becoming in terms of our own Divine Nature.

By turning our attention inside to our true God-Selves, we are illuminating our virtues and talents. This illumination also exposes our shadows. Once we transform the energy, we change our relationships and our lives to reflect our new selves. When we grow in Self love through self-awareness, we draw people into our lives that are kind and beneficial to the nature and purpose of who we are. We have peace in our lives.

The blame and victim games are coming to a screeching halt. We know at some level, we've created these relationships and experiences to evolve. We are taking responsibility for our lives. It's time.

The patterns and cycles of destructive energy projection through hate, greed, aggression, control, deception, and coercion are ending. We don't resist or emanate the same energy patterns, or behavior that we clearly see is hurtful and damaging. The new energy of the New World doesn't allow it. When we don't "get it" our lessons become harsher and harsher and our cyclical energy return gets faster and faster and more intensified.

As we contemplate our experience within, in the space of deep compassion, we are getting the blessing of the lesson and we have new awareness. When we incorporate that awareness into our being with practice, we grow into it and expand our Selves. Mentally we practice with songs, chants, affirmations, or self-talk reminders. Physically we practice by taking action through our behavior. Emotionally we test our awareness about how we feel after "showing up," using that awareness in a new life experience. As we project our energy through our thoughts, emotions, and actions in a new way, our experiences improve to create a more joyful and happy life.

Reflection awareness is serving us to become conscious of our own Divinity. As we are evolving at quickening paces, we are creating more and more positive experiences that create the feelings around ourselves and our lives that we enjoy. Ultimately, what we are trying to create is happiness through positive feelings. When we are vigilant with the projection of positive feelings without denying negative feelings that help us to grow, we reach a new level of consciousness and soul growth. That's what we're here for. Reflection Awareness is a huge blessing.

The consciousness of unconditional love is changing the world. From the seed of self-love to the love of humanity, our capacity to understand, to give, and to receive love is expanding. Our experiences are becoming rich with love and gratitude. We see ourselves in others when we are willing to face the truth of our True Selves. As we consciously focus on the good in others, we illuminate who they are and who we are as One bright star.

We live in joy in our New World because we have used Reflection Awareness to transform ourselves and our world. We are deeply grateful for the challenging opportunities we have been given to awaken and discover our Greater Self. Thank God.

Freedom

Freedom rests in our mind.
We can claim it in its totality in any moment.

We can claim global freedom by using directed
synergized group consciousness focused on solutions.

Freedom is Free

When we empty our mind from which we create
We can choose a new scene with a brand new slate
In our imagination we can dream what we desire
All things are possible when love is on fire

When all beliefs are suspended removing limitation
We enjoy the freedom of our own creation
We have free will and can stand our ground
We can use freedom of mind no matter who's around

The passion of love from our soul through our heart
Is the energy we use to find our life's part
This connection once found and secured in place
Is infinite and free though we don't see a trace

We each have a blueprint for the life that we live
We take life from God and choose what we give
When we surrender to Life and discover our calling
Freedom follows to create any gift without stalling

When we stop and focus our attention inside
And get totally present with all senses open wide
We imagine with love as joy shines on our face
We get what we want in our own little place

If we can really believe in our dreams come true
Life will follow suit in our outer view
All we have to do is nothing—just be
It doesn't cost anything, freedom is free

Breaking out of Boxes

Nothing is the same anymore. Nothing. As much as we try, and some of us are trying awfully hard, we can't fit into any of the old boxes anymore. Even if we fit, the box is not serving its purpose; it's all for naught. The work boxes, the religion boxes, the relationship boxes, the political boxes, educational boxes; all the boxes that we've created are disintegrating. That's because it was based on the old paradigm and the old paradigm way of living based on material reality is breaking down. Rapidly. The new paradigm way of living is emerging. It is based on the freedom and expression of Spirit.

We can express Divine love by reclaiming our own personal freedom and honoring the freedom of others. By using the power of our creative will, we can live any way we choose. We can eliminate our false perceptions that keep us in jail. Then we can eliminate outer manifestations of power and control. Whether parental, institutional, governmental, or commercial, these perceived sanctions against our freedom are really disintegrating in their power. When they are in alignment with the highest good of all, they are serving their purpose. However, many people have abused positions of power due to ill intentions, ignorance, or greed. Their time is up.

Once people reclaim their freedom, they just do what they want within the realm of Universal law. It's that simple. Do you want more freedom? It's yours to claim.

Our individual freedom is protected by Universal law. It's the Divine law of souls that ensures Cosmic order. It is against Universal law to take free will away from others through the use of control or force. Now that we are emerging as responsible souls, we take into account the energetic balance that takes place if we harm others. We do have complete freedom. When we operate with an awareness of being part of the whole life system, we realize our energy cycles right back to us. If we choose to have positive experiences, we express positive energy. When we express love, peace and cooperation, we experience the same positive expressions from others and feel even more unity. If we express fear, power, and control, we experience difficulties and painful life experiences in return and experience even more separation.

Those old boxes of relationships that still contain energies of control or expectation are no longer working. We are now experiencing more freedom within our relationships, or we are exiting them.

When we truly love another, we give them the total freedom to be who they are, and we still love them. That's how God loves us. He and She gave us free will. Is there any withholding of love on the part of God, no matter how we use our free will? Absolutely not!

It is so important during these times to grant our spouses, partners, friends, family, and co-workers the freedom to express their free will. Let them make their own choices. Refrain from judgment, telling them what to do, or expecting them to do what you want them to do. If you don't let people experience the freedom of making their own personal choices according to their free will, they may feel pressured and leave the relationship. If someone is pressuring you too much, remember you always have options to find full expression of your free will.

Everybody has choices. They may be based on the choices of others, but as we are becoming ever more true to ourselves, we know when it is time to make choices that enable and empower us to express ourselves freely. We are free to be who we are and to choose relationships that support us in exercising our free will.

We're not fitting into the old boxes of work, either. People are dropping out of the rat race in large numbers. We are not happy unless we are earning a living according to our passion. We are using our free will to express our creative energies doing what we love. We are discovering our life purpose, or individual reason for living. We want meaningful work with purpose. We care and we want to contribute. We are getting more and more determined to do only what brings us joy in life. If that means decorating houses instead of going to an office, then we are making our plans and executing them. We are free to choose our creative expression.

Financial fears around this are becoming a thing of the past. It may seem like the opposite if you're not on the other side yet. Once you notice more and more people are taking the plunge and making it, you can gather your courage and set yourself free!

No matter what our religious practice, whether we even have one or not, we are all becoming unified with the love that is God. Although many wars have been fought over the righteousness of one religion over another, the real truth that love is the basis of all religions is emerging. Doctrines and dogma only serve mankind when they inspire God's love within each and every heart.

Many religious institutions are dissolving barriers to work with other religions toward world peace and harmony. We are using God's love constructively and providing interfaith services. We are demonstrating how we can share and serve each other while practicing our own faith. We are looking at what is the same about differing faiths, and sharing to create a new evolved synthesis that is deepening and expanding love. God is happy about that.

Love is about harmony and unity, not about discord and separation. We are holding the position in unity consciousness that there doesn't have to be only one right. We can all be right and share the richness of diversity in our cultures and religions. We are now loving all other humans and accepting their free will to serve and worship God according to their own choice. We are free to worship in our own fashion, and at the same time, people of all religions are experiencing the desire for brotherhood. Notice the cooperative inter-faith worship services and events taking place. Notice the increase in the level of voluntary community service. Now we are free to celebrate our true unity born of love. Love is taking action to help another, and that is the brotherhood that is being expressed in our New World.

So many kids just do not fit into the old educational boxes any more. For many years, we grew up going to school receiving passed down knowledge, beliefs, and distorted stories from all the years before us. Children have been herded into classrooms where there is too much curriculum taught by creative rote at best and evaluations in the form of written tests have been prevalent. The trend toward alternative education has picked up momentum. Creative teachers within the schools are touching lives in their own unique way by sharing their wisdom. Home schooling, private schools, and charter schools have been helping to bridge the way to our new educational paradigm. New trends in schools where creative abilities are tapped, ethics are taught, and the value of self-awareness is inspired, are emerging. Schools are making way for peace and love-based values awareness such as non-violent communication programs to give our youth the opportunity to be models of integrity.

The new education of today is inspiring joy in the hearts of children. They are being guided to find their own unique gifts and talents. They are encouraged to explore the vast opportunities in the world to find what they love. They enjoy creative expression according to their own free will. They are being pointed toward and expressing their own genius. They realize compassion for others is a higher road than feeding their own ego. They are expressing their innocent honesty and authenticity.

We are realizing the tables have been turned. The children are our teachers. They deserve their freedom and our encouragement and our full support.

In addition to formal education, the cultural education handed down by our friends, family, and institutions is outdated and is being replaced. We are in the process of unlearning many of the once believed myths that limited our scope of possibilities. We're getting rid of the "shoulds" and accepting what is true and real. Instead of acting how we "should" act, we are revealing our true feelings. As adults, we have a lot more to unlearn than our youth.

Commercialism is disintegrating because we have broken out of those boxes. They had us going though, that's for sure! We bought into the "shoulds" of designer clothes, the status of jewelry, shapes of our bodies, youthful appearance, what we paid attention to for entertainment, and fads of all kinds. Now that we have changed our value system and know that happiness is not about how we look or things we have, but about sharing and caring, we are laughing at ourselves! But we are showing up as natural, just being ourselves, without the need to present an image of being or having this or that to realize our personal self-worth. We are concerned with who we are, rather than what we have.

In our New World, life is simpler and much more enjoyable. We feel so much lighter because we realize that what brings us the most pleasure is free. Nature is free. Love is free. Freedom is free.

Security

Inner confidence and trust in receiving life's provisions.

In our New World this is realized through a system of unified cooperation of caring and sharing inner and outer resources.

Feeling Abundance

Security is a feeling of having plenty to live
It emanates from inside as we feel free to give
We share what we have and know there's enough for all
We are our brothers' keepers, life's true protocol

Our abundance of food served with love's preparation
Is masterfully distributed throughout every nation
Food from gardens throughout our community
We cook for our neighbors and celebrate unity

We trade our skills, creations, our extras and such
Not a human on earth does poverty touch
The opulence of God's bounty is shared with great joy
With dignity and pride our talents we employ

By sharing and trading we're not hooked on money
The feeling of caring in our hearts makes us sunny
We're shining with love as we share and cooperate
Our past commercial values we liberate

We are free to live as naturally as we please
We have a bountiful lifestyle, one of ease
We create from our hearts with pure creativity
We choose and love each activity

Our new security is as stable as our inner love
We feel it inside; it fits like a glove
With full trust we receive abundant provisions
The energy we share comes back with precision

New Security

One major viewpoint that has shifted is that security is all about money. People used to feel secure if they had saved for retirement, had plenty of savings or investments, or had plenty of income to pay their monthly expenses. If you are open to shifting your viewpoint, you may feel more secure now, and as the destiny of our world unfolds.

Money has been elevated in our minds by programmed beliefs. We have been lead to believe our very self worth is based on how much money we have or can generate. We get evaluated and judged by how much money we appear to have. Some people who buy into this value system create their appearance to reflect a certain amount of wealth to gain a sense of status.

Everybody knows we don't take anything material with us when we die. And yet, so many lives are concerned with the accumulation of wealth or status based on money.

It is Who we Are that really counts. The only thing we take with us when we leave our earthly bodies is our innermost selves—our True Selves. Life is eternal. As individual souls, we live on and on. The real value in life is how much better we are at the end of it all.

We are waking up to what's real on all fronts. We have to now. The world is changing. It is time right now to realize what **real security** is and to develop it within our lives.

Real security comes from **caring** and **sharing**.

By dropping all judgments and seeing all people as children of God, we notice we are all the same. We all eat, go to the bathroom, clothe our bodies, seek shelter, and seek to share love with others. We realize that we all have our challenges. Life is prompting us to grow and become better. As souls, we are all growing up together.

We are all doing the best we can. We all make our decisions in life based on what we know to be our own truth about life.

How can we judge another's choices when we don't share their experiences, their perspective? A simple way to get out of judgment is to just realize everyone has their own reasons to be or do whatever they choose. Just because you know better than to do something, doesn't mean they do. Have patience, the way you would with your own child.

It is human to err, but eventually we all discover our own Divinity within. This is the process of Life. Let's help each other along the way. Let's feel secure knowing that we are there to understand, to care, and to share.

We all have something of ourselves to give. We can each contribute to life by helping others. Each of us can just go into the depths of our own hearts in quiet moments and ask, "What can I do to help others?" "Who can I help?" It doesn't matter if we help many people or just one. It doesn't matter if we give a lot or a little.

When we come from our heart, we can feel that we truly have a lot to give. A kind word, a listening ear, or a smile, are simple things that show we care. We can give away things we no longer need to those who do need them. We can do a chore or run an errand for someone. We can be there for friends, neighbors, or loved ones when they are ill. We can lighten each other's load.

All of us have unique talents and gifts to share. One may share food from their garden, another a song from their heart. Still another may write a poem or paint a picture. In these gifts from the soul, we receive our deepest pleasures. We reach the fulfillment of our hearts, both as giver and receiver.

Giving and receiving appreciation is as precious as gold. Kids are really good at this. That's why so many great people have given their lives as teachers. It is common knowledge that teachers receive very low salaries compared to most professions. The true value of education has not yet been realized, but teachers continue to give their energies for our youth because they care. They receive more joy from the appreciation of children than anything money could ever buy them. That's something to ponder, isn't it? We could help others by really striving to express appreciation for each other more.

From the small things to the large, when we attune to our own Divinity and express a growing concern for others and act out of compassion, we can grow our level of caring and sharing. In return, we feel a great sense of security. We feel a sense of true inner value and we know we will be taken care of, too.

This inner knowingness is built around trust in God—the God of our own hearts where our True Self exists. It is full reliance on God, our Father, who is greater than each one of us, but knows and cares for every individual soul. Communion with God within our hearts helps us to know that this is so. Giving our love and attention to God helps us to tune in and feel God's love and compassion for us. This is our unlimited Source. This is where we receive the energy of love and compassion for ourselves, and as our cup runneth over, we have plenty to give to others.

God is also our Divine Mother who caresses our soul with comfort. One of the most healing acts we can do for ourselves is to take a walk in nature and ask God for comfort. As we breathe deeply, the energy of pure love and healing washes over our being. It feels like a love bath. We feel not only comforted, but renewed in spirit. When we feel energetically drained, frustrated with life, or low in spirit for any reason, we can renew our spirit by caring for ourselves. Whether we walk in nature, take a hot bubble bath with candles, listen to soft music while resting, or meditate, or do whatever it is that makes us feel better, we can renew our spirits and gain the energy we need to help ourselves and others.

When we care and share out of compassion, we are not only helping others, but we are helping ourselves on so many levels. First of all, spiritually, energetically, we are all one. We help our larger Self of which we are all a part.

Second of all, we help our individual self as all that we give comes back to us, multiplied. If we deliver our energy of self constructively and positively toward life, life returns positive and constructive feelings and experiences. If we are negative with our actions and emotions, we receive the same back. Even if we don't notice the cause and effect relationships, we can be certain that life is fair.

In fact, life can be better than fair. If we ask for Divine guidance and assistance, grace and assistance comes our way. We can be forgiven when we err, and we can get better. We can BE better. We can learn to forgive more readily, too.

Just remember that God is in each of our hearts, ready to love and assist us in every moment. When we love God, we feel love pour into our being. We can tap into the endless Source of Divine love and feel secure in every moment.

When we tap into our Source, which is God, and then become our true Divine Selves through caring and sharing, we have the strongest sense of security that there is. This is true security. When we realize our own Divinity and express our own unique inherent virtues and talents, life can be supreme, no matter what is going on in the world. Remember that always.

Abundance

True abundance is a deep sense of fulfillment.
It is the satisfaction of the heart's only desire—love.

It's Already Here

If you're looking for anything
There's no reason to fear
Look inside, you'll see
That it's already here

Believe it or not
The truth of your being
Is making up
Everything that you're seeing

Whatever it is
You wish to have or give
With love and vision
It's what you can live

What about love
The special person for me?
Inside there is love
Just let it be

Let it blossom
As you express who you are
Your love will attract them
You won't have to go far

What about material
Things that I need?
Look inside
And plant the seed

Feel the feeling
Picture that you have it
It will come right to you
Reach out and grab it

Trust God in your heart
To supply every need
There's plenty for all
No reason for greed

Feel your abundance
Be of good cheer
Express deep gratitude
That it's already here

Opening the Door to Heaven
with the Key of Gratitude

As we express heartfelt appreciation for our gifts of Life to God, we expand to the realm of infinite possibilities as creators. When we acknowledge God as our Source of everything we are, everything we do, and everything we have, we are humble. We receive more. We also have more to give.

When we are in a state of gratitude as we are in our still, silent moments creating consciously, we are very present in the eternal moment of Now. We are consciously present with God. We really know and deeply feel that we really are co-creating with God. We truly accept the fact that we were made in the likeness and image of God and use our God powers to move mountains of energy into our beloved forms.

Gratitude opens our hearts to receive more and to give more. As we contemplate our lives with a sense of appreciation, we more fully comprehend our blessings. Especially when we look upon our challenges with gratitude, do we open ourselves to the blessings and lessons that they contain. It opens the space for creative solutions to enter our hearts and minds. We are inspired and uplifted. We have the tools to open all doors and flow with life.

As we love even our most challenging situations and most painful feelings, we release their wisdom and transform the energy. What is left is awareness embodied as wisdom, and energy to use to create new, more joyful forms. We are healed and have evolved in the process. We are left with only blessings to appreciate, and a lighter and more joyful feeling toward ourselves and others.

Every person's soul who receives our feelings, thoughts, words, and actions of appreciation brightens who they are. They feel our love. They get inspired to do more for us, for others, and for themselves. The deep intrinsic value of genuine appreciation is priceless. It is a gift of immeasurable proportions because it touches who we are at our very core.

Acts of Self-love help us to appreciate ourselves more, too. They are gifts of appreciation to our soul. They are gifts to God. Loving ourselves brightens the God, or good, in us and we naturally shine and express our talents and virtues more fully. We express joy as we create and play in life. And when we communicate our true feelings, we feel gratitude to ourselves for being authentic, living in integrity. Our full expression of essence leads to a deep sense of fulfillment. This is the feeling of gratitude for life—for experiencing True Self expression—really living in joy in the natural flow of life.

The essence of nature, beautiful and abundant, generously shares the pure essence of loving intelligence. We are grateful for the conscious energy exchange with all of life on our planet. We are supplied with abundant resources from Mother Earth. We feel supported in every way. We are so grateful; we are giving back and taking care of her much more consciously.

We now realize how vitally important it is to feel and express gratitude. It is a form of service that every one of us performs in our daily life to an ever-increasing degree. The process of contemplating creative forms of showing appreciation increases our motivation and ability to give abundant appreciation. We experience the joy of giving.

We are increasingly becoming more and giving more. As we love our Selves and what we have in the moment, the more brilliant and expansive is our light. We are now feeling deep gratitude in every moment as we receive and express an abundance of love. Love never felt so good as it does now. It is deep, warm, comforting, secure, reliable, soft, pure, and natural. It is real, lasting, eternal.

Recognizing love as the Source of what we create, we imagine that we already have what we desire. As we receive this love with gratitude, we have found the secret to manifesting all of our hearts desires in the now moment. The love from our hearts is married to the light of our mind, and we are truly free to create.

This pure Divine love that we are receiving in gratitude, expressing and sharing, fills our hearts with such joy! We have a lot to be grateful for, especially each other. We are using the key of gratitude to open Heaven's door to let the light shine in and through us. We are shining bright with gratitude in our New World!

Evolution

For whatever we do with our lives, whatever we have,
whatever places or people we experience, at the end of it all,
what we have left is what we have become.

That's our soul's evolution.
It is the ultimate reason for living.

Nothing But Angels

The souls that walk among us and touch our very lives
Though disguised as imperfect humans, they open up our eyes
The effect they have upon us is no less than divinely inspired
For these are the angels of God from which we have inquired

As we delve inside and ask God about life and what to do
Our answers come from All That Is, the souls of humans, too
It is these very people on who we try out our expressions
Subjecting themselves to any behavior; allowing for our lesson

Our lesson is the feeling we get that tells us if we are in tune with our soul
If we express from love, then we have reached our goal
But no matter what we do, they are here in the room with us
These angelic human creatures whose divine mission we can trust

Sometimes angels have a way of creating undesirable drama
But we can step aside and be observers without creating karma
As they provide opportunity for us to be more clear on who we are
We can hone our expressions from reactive to creative and bless them from afar

The angels that we keep close to us still keep us alert all the same
They love us and they challenge us as we play our human game
Through sharing life's experiences of fun and joy and laughter
We make up how we choose to live; knowing it's evolution we're after

As we realize these people are angels in our lives
We feel the expression of God's love and look beyond their disguise
As our eyes open up and our Awareness increases
We notice we are one in spirit; not just individual pieces

Instead of feeling the misery of illusion we now feel the joy of unity and love
We know we are here for each other to create the dream that life is made of
As we maintain our sense of Oneness and express the love that we are
We thank God for the angels in our lives and enjoy life more by far

That's Progress!

While we are consciously evolving, it's extremely beneficial to remind ourselves—and each other—about all of the progress we have made. Take a moment now...just pause...and go inside to review your many accomplishments. Contemplate everything from new awareness that has not been fully instilled into your being, to full-blown outer accomplishments in behavioral/personality improvements and goals you have reached. You have come a long way, baby! Congratulations!!!

****

It is natural to desire changes for the better in ourselves and our lives. It is natural to desire anything, but as we evolve our desires change. Even they evolve.

Earlier in our evolution, before we were consciously evolving, we used to change due to crises, or trial and error. Sometimes we repeated the same destructive patterns over and over and over until we got it. Now that we are awake, we are evolving so much faster. It's easier, too, since we've developed processes for change.

Divine Intervention has also help to ease and speed up the process. When we ask God or our Angels or Ascended Masters to help us, we receive guidance and tools that vastly help our endeavors to evolve. By using Oneness Awareness, we know we are connected to all beings on all realms. We have help at every level. We are realizing this more and more, and using their Divine guidance and assistance.

We are using our precious Life Energy more constructively, and we each have the Freedom to walk our own path, do it our own way.

Friends and family, or Earth Angels, also assist us in so many ways. Knowing we are connected, we are all dedicated to helping each other.

Best of all, now that we consciously employ our Higher Self, or God-Self, to direct our consciousness according to God's will, we find so much deep compassion for ourselves as we evolve. We know we are perfect in every moment, because we are in the perfect process called Life.

When babies are born, we revel in their perfection, don't we? And yet we know, they will learn a lot in this lifetime. No matter where we are on our journey, we realize that we are attempting to constantly get better and consistently live the truth from our life lessons in our ever-evolving beingness.

There is no failure. There are no mistakes that do not become blessings. Every experience has its merit. It's just a matter of time before we realize the wisdom we are gaining from our life experiences, and now it is much faster since we are consciously looking at life through self-awareness.

We may get discouraged at times, but even that fades away with self-compassion and Divine Mercy. Just a change of perception along life's course can always bring us back to the realization of the perfection of each moment or circumstance.

We have learned to be vigilant regarding our thoughts, feelings, words, and actions. Now that we know we are creating in every moment, we watch ourselves like a hawk! We don't feel like creating any more misery for ourselves, do we? Now that we have become aware that we, ourselves, are responsible for creating our lives and all of the experiences therein, we are using that awareness to make our dreams come true. Isn't it wonderful?

Truth is eternal and the wisdom that has been revealed throughout the ages has always been available to aid us in our evolutionary process. In this awakening stage of humanity, there are so many Paradigm Pioneers, those that have paved the way to personal transformation. These are the Lightworkers that came to serve in these rapid evolutionary times. They are givers that find joy in serving. They are appreciated beyond measure.

All of us are helping each other and "turning up the love," as I like to phrase it. Let's pat ourselves, and each other, on the back, and keep on keeping on.

We have evolved into a humanity of Brotherhood, unified by our hearts. If it seems that someone has not evolved into loving and creative expressions, lets just keep loving them as they find their way. Let's follow Jesus' example and take the attitude: "Forgive them, for they know not what they do." By changing ourselves, we are changing the mass consciousness of society. As we reach the critical mass, there will be celebration indeed!

Let's envision the world as if everyone were awake now, being their highest potential, and loving each other in a variety of creative ways.

This IS our New World. Thanks for helping to create it.

Acceptance

Please accept me the way I am.

Everyone

The Key of Acceptance

All the doors of life open when we have the key
When we accept one another unconditionally
In our hearts we truly understand
We're here to love and lend a hand

Acceptance opens the door for love to flow through
We learn to love others, no matter what they do
When accepting everyone for who they are
We see each person as a shining star

When love from our heart enters our mind
Understanding is born making us kind
When the wisdom of understanding flows through our heart
Out flows compassion for us to impart

Compassion is the energy of love and wisdom
Awareness of Oneness brings universal vision
With this vision we can all cooperate
To create peace now without having to wait

The peace that is born from this understanding
Is what we've been yearning, what our souls are demanding
Once fulfilled within each one
It shines on all just like the sun

The energy of compassion brings about healing
Now we can all be honest with our feelings
This is not the time for peace to compromise
But to see the love within all eyes

Universal Vision

When we truly understand the underlying Oneness of Spirit and that we are each expressing God in our own way, we can relax in life. We can accept our selves and others in each moment. We can accept the "isness" of any given situation or circumstance and live peacefully. We can grow into this awareness by realizing we are each responsible only for our individual part—our own life and our own unique expression.

Life is a perfect process, constantly changing and evolving. Our own lives are constantly changing and we are constantly evolving as individuals. We know that for everything we do, we have a reason. Even if we err, we understand why. Not that the reason is an excuse for harmful effects, but the understanding helps bring about acceptance.

Mistakes are the realization that we could have made a higher choice. We often regret decisions that bring about undesired results. In the perfection of life, so-called mistakes bring about a new awareness. We catch ourselves faster and faster and change our ways when we have opened to a new awareness. As perfection would have it, Divine purpose is served. The process is changing us for the better. We evolve.

Using mistakes as tools of evolution helps us to accept ourselves and others more readily. Using self-reflection, we look directly at ourselves and say: "I understand and accept myself just the way I am." This places us at ease in each now moment. From there we can decide to make changes--gently, with lots of compassion and love.

By securing our spiritual connection with our soul through silence or meditation, we can attune to our own talents and virtues and let them flow naturally. They can flush out any impurities or blockages that are in the way. Accept that the process of life is perfect and total acceptance of life brings inner peace.

Since we are only aware of our own perspective in totality, and our own qualities and weaknesses, we need not be concerned with trying to judge or change anyone else. That is up to them.

By modeling our own perception of what is right and true for us by standing in our own truth and integrity, we may have an impact on others, but it is their free will choice to be who they choose to be. Our choice, if we don't like someone, is to create proximity of relationship that suits our resonation with them.

Total acceptance, however, creates a space for each person to be who they are in the moment. It opens the door to understanding and paves the way to love. It actually gives them room to grow.

We are all transforming right now. We are all learning a new way of life. By accepting and understanding each other and the process of life, we achieve a deeper sense of connection. This brings us into unity, into wholeness.

Since we really are connected to the same Source, God, we begin to see what God has in store for us as we mature and transcend old ways. We see that we are becoming a race of souls who harmonize with each other and live in peace. We begin to glimpse the Universal Vision, one by one, until we all share it. As we hold this vision together, we begin to live it.

It all starts with acceptance.

With pure imagination and love in our hearts, we see the Peaceful Paradise that is forming into our reality. With integrity and purity of being, we are manifesting the Universal Vision. This is our New World.

Kindness

"Kindness is my religion."

Dalai Lama

Conscious Kindness

For those unaware
Thoughtfulness lacks
Deeply hurting us
Turning their backs

Because they know
Not what they do
Forgiveness bestowed
Heals them and you

Contemplating others
As heart is in pieces
I know I've fallen short
Awareness increases

Gratitude expressed
Growing inside
Vow to do better
Creates inner pride

Universe of order
Instills accountability
Eventually waking up
Taking responsibility

Open to God
Compassion that heals
Warming my heart
How much better it feels

Intent to become
Consciously kind
Expressing God's love
Opens heart and mind

Kindness Counts

Sometimes we have experiences that create deep hurtful feelings within us. If we get quiet and really get in tune with our feelings, especially when they are strong, they have much wisdom within them.

Inner wisdom, when paid attention to, helps us to respond to any person or circumstance from the highest level of awareness. We develop a deep understanding of ourselves and also of others. There is no blame on either end, just a total understanding of different perspectives. This understanding inspires love. Love for ourselves heals us and help us to totally accept ourselves and at the same time causing us to grow to new levels of awareness.

We are also inspired to love others. We realize that they are acting according to their own understanding of life. Often, when others hurt us, it is just a case of being unconscious of their effects on us. Rarely are others intentionally hurting us, and if it seems that way, it's really just a cover up for trying to fulfill something that is missing in their own life. They mistakenly feel that they can, in effect, steal what you have for themselves. They eventually learn that life doesn't work that way.

Once understanding is experienced within, we can easily forgive any word or action. Because of the depth of our understanding, we realize there is really nothing to forgive since the genesis of their actions come from a place of unknowingness. Communication with the intent to understand each other is appropriate and healing.

If someone repeatedly hurts us out of their own unconsciousness, we can make choices that will alleviate these circumstances. One way is to disassociate one's self from them and create a space for healing. Disassociation also allows space for the others to learn their lessons. The time frame of the disassociation depends on the nature and intent of the relationship. It also depends on the dynamics of the relationship, such as the willingness of each person to grow through challenges. If the intent of the relationship is to last a lifetime, then the disassociation may be just enough time to allow space for healing. Sometimes healing takes a lifetime. Our spirit lets us know what is appropriate in each specific case.

When we are consciously evolving, we look even deeper. We look at our own words and actions to find where there's room for improvement. We ask ourselves, "Who have I hurt unconsciously?" "Who may I be hurting now?" Then we resolve to make new choices with that new level of awareness. We are using life as a reflection for our own evolution, its ultimate purpose. Then we find how we can show up better and treat others in our life with the utmost in consideration.

Everyone is ultimately just seeking happiness. We all do what we think of in the moment that will make us happy. Truly, it is lasting inner joy that we seek, not the state of mind that we call happy. First of all, a state of mind is a choice and we can easily manipulate that with our thoughts. Secondly, rather than temporary pleasures that we can grasp in the moment, a long term thinker would realize that lasting happiness, or inner joy, is found with deep inner experiences balanced with pleasant outer experiences, creating precious moments for ourselves and whoever is in our space.

Wisdom derived from within increases our awareness and helps us to evolve into better human beings. In fact, we change our very soul. That's what we came here to do. We use relationships to see how we can show up and make increasingly better choices. As we practice these better choices, it changes who we are. We evolve at the soul level and consistently show up as being kind and considerate. We learn how critical it is to love ourselves in that way as well. We reflect God's unconditional love.

We all have different scopes in terms of self. Those who have a very small sense of self tend to seek their own egoic happiness without realizing the full implications of our inherent Oneness. Because of their lack of understanding, they don't consider their behavioral impact on others. One who is conscious of being part of the whole tunes in to the feelings of others and sets the intention to be consciously kind. We develop our kindness when we always understand that people are doing the best they can and are having their own life challenges that they came here to resolve.

By practicing life with an intent of being kind to everyone, we develop a universal kindness. This is evidence of an evolved soul. This universal kindness, once grasped by the masses of Earth's inhabitants, will create a world where we can all experience harmonious peace and joy equally. We will consistently feel the love of God through each other.

Listening

Hear the silence, feel my love.

Listening to Life

Silence...
Listen to awareness

Hear...
God's voice in all of life

Breathe...
Divine inspiration

Feel...
Passion of heart

Observe...
Doors that are open

Welcome...
Truth from all Sources

Vigilance...
For synchronicity

Intuit...
Feel truth of knowing

Sense...
Essence of energy

Understand...
Other's perspectives

Accept...
Feelings as real

Listen...
With all senses

Trust...
All is perfect

Those Who Have Ears

Although we ultimately count on our own inner guidance to know truth, if we are open to listening, we can continually grow. The more we listen, the faster we grow. The faster we grow, the easier life becomes.

Being present with God, or sitting in deep meditation, can bring us to the Unified field of consciousness that contains all answers to life. Keeping this spiritual ear open allows us to increase our intuition. Paying attention to our intuition also helps it to grow stronger. We are all realizing that taking time just to "be" in the stillness of our hearts opens us up to receive the love of who we are and prepares us for full True Self expression.

Many times we get answers directly from our still, small voice. However, sometimes we ask questions from this inner place and get answers from outside. Sometimes the answers come from songs, books, or through the voice of humans. They can come from anywhere. If we are open, we can hear the message. If we believe we already have all the answers, we don't hear the message. If we believe the piece of truth we have is the whole truth, we don't hear the message.

For me, I believe everyone has something to teach me. I listen keenly. Sometimes what I hear resonates with me, I feel it as truth, and sometimes it doesn't. Sometimes I ponder it or take it into meditation. I discern between personal truth or belief, and Universal truth.

When we speak our truth, sometimes people listen and sometimes they don't. Their ears may be closed because they believe they already know the full answer. Each of us has a part of the truth. Each of us has our own perspective. It is in sharing our perspectives that our awareness expands. Just being willing to listen to everybody, really listen with the intent to understand, without judgment of age, race, culture, appearance, religious or political beliefs, opens our ears.

It is this understanding of knowing that each person has an awareness of some valid truth from their perspective that I call Pixel Consciousness. Each point of light on a computer screen is a pixel. All of the points make up the whole picture. Each of the points could surmise their own color or luminosity and say, "this is how it is." Each of them is right, so there's no need to argue just because one pixel has another color or different attributes.

There is some element of truth that is unique to each perspective. A point of view by be colored by beliefs that may not be true, but with discernment we can glean the truth. When our intuition has become keen through meditation, it becomes increasingly easier to discern what is ultimate truth.

Some things are pure and not subject to argument. Look for the "isness." For example, you cannot argue with another person's feelings. Feelings are what they are and they always contain wisdom. Although there may be misunderstanding that provoked the feelings, the feelings are still real.

Communication is paramount to obtaining understanding and discovering truth. As long as we stay with each other in clear, calm communication, we can create win-win situations. Everyone can be right, and everyone can win. We can all grow from the truth and feel the love flow as understanding blossoms.

Now we are all becoming open to gleaning the truth from listening to each other's perspective and we are each becoming richer in awareness by this mutual sharing.

When we have Pixel Consciousness and listen with open hearts, we have ears.

Understanding

All other possibilities aside,
understanding is the best gift we can give,
to ourselves and to one another.

Life Goes On

Life goes on and on
Though changes we endure
We process as we adjust each time
And we become more pure

Many moments to enjoy
Through essence of our feeling
This is what we rely on
It makes life more appealing

Sometimes we judge others
For something that they do
Then later on in our lives
We do the same thing, too

Peace of mind is more stable
When we understand
To love them just the way they are
And lend a helping hand

And if we really listen
To what each other has to say
Then we can really understand them
Our hearts can touch that way

We learn more about life
As we love throughout our days
The choices that we make
Construct our lives this way

We create our own experiences
We make it up as we go along
Trying to understand always
Helps us never to go wrong

Dedicated to God in all of us!

Knowing Without Knowing

Upon developing a Universal understanding of life, we know that each person behaves out of their own current conception of life, and each person is doing the best they can with their life according to their soul's state of evolution and awareness of Life principles. Understanding goes beyond acceptance because we know there is a purpose behind each person's way of being; a purpose behind their words and actions. Even rote habits begin with a cause from within each individual person that that is in place to serve that soul's purpose. Whether we agree or not is not an issue. Whether we think we know better or not is not an issue.

When Jesus said: "Forgive them, for they know not what they do" he was coming from this deep understanding of Life. He knew that if his persecutors realized the cyclical nature of personal energy, they wouldn't use their Life energy destructively. He knew there was a lack of Oneness awareness and the implications of the unified Greater Self that we share as Children of God. We know that within Universal Law personal Life energy is ultimately balanced: "as ye sow; so shall ye reap." The application of this awareness around being understanding yields understanding back to us.

Instantaneous forgiveness is actually not forgiveness at all, but a display of compassionate understanding and mercy. It is trusting in the perfect Divine process of Life.

We've all had experiences where we may have judged another for a certain thing, and then later on did the same thing. At that point we realized what it was like to be in the experience and knew full well our personal reasons for doing it. We've also had experiences where we may have inflicted personal pain or damage from a certain type of act, and then we ended up on the other side of the same type of experience, playing the opposite role. This balance creates an understanding that we instill within ourselves as knowledge that we apply in life to experience as wisdom.

Furthermore, when we observe a friend or family member doing something, we know them, so we tend to have some level of understanding that may eliminate criticism or judgment. On the other hand, when a stranger, someone we don't know or barely know, does the same thing, we may lean toward criticizing their lack of judgment or common sense. For example, let's say you are driving and following your brother who is trying to find a new address to a car repair shop. He drives slow and makes mistakes and has to turn around, or gets in the wrong lane or something. You exercise patience and understanding because you know he doesn't know where he is going. Other drivers may honk and lose their patience because they don't know why he's driving so crazy. Sometimes we are those other drivers.

Everybody has a reason to be how they are, or do what they do. And, we have all made mistakes—sometimes they are silly blunders, and sometimes they are grave errors. Such are the experiences of life that contain our lessons.

With this awareness applied in our daily lives, we expand our understanding and we don't have to know why people are the way they are, or do what they do. We just know they have their reasons and we understand without knowing the specific reason.

With this higher-level perspective of understanding, we are open to giving unconditional love, the greatest change agent in the world. Unconditional love is the most fertile ground for the seed of consciousness. It naturally releases what is not like it, and becomes its full potential.

If we set a conscious intention to be unconditional love, anything that is not unconditional love in our being will emerge and be purified. We realize we must first unconditionally love ourselves, know and speak our truth, set our boundaries, and realize our personal value through inner awareness. Knowing our Self and becoming true to our Self-become foundational in being unconditional love since love is truth expressed fully. It takes courage to live in full integrity as unconditional love, but the rewards are eternal. Inner strength grows, consciousness expands, spiritual gifts are bestowed, and the soul is fulfilled.

When we tune into God's unconditional love, we thrive. We master our Life energy with wisdom and live from pure essence. Our spirit sprouts into a unique creative flower in the garden of Life. When we administer unconditional love upon others, it gives them a chance to discover themselves freely, and become the best that they can be in every moment. With unconditional love, we can see their potential, and help them to see it, too.

We are now applying and expanding a deeper level of understanding. We have gained wisdom from a variety of life experiences that have given us the foundation to understand each other and have compassion. As we accumulate wisdom from our life lessons, we can share our understanding of life with each other.

And now, in our New World, with open hearts and minds, we can consciously exchange our enlightened energy to incorporate the understanding and wisdom from each other.

Compassion

Compassion supercedes any mental notion that may inhibit love's flow.
It is the direct realization and expression of pure love.

Heavy Heart

Heavy heart
Magnitudinous feelings
Outer havoc
Inner reeling

Opening wide
Sacred heart place
Creating wider
Personal love space

Feeling pain
Intense desire
What solution
One inquires

Love comes forth
Magically
From God, through us
Dependably

We expand
We now love more
Expressing love
Forevermore

Feeling for Others

Compassion is the healing, transformative aspect of love. It is the love a mother has for its child. It is deep, unconditional, caring, and motivated to act. This motivation comes in the form of helping, loving through affection, serving in any way possible to elevate the feelings and experience of another. There are no barriers to the flow of love when it reaches the level of compassion. Its very existence changes all in its vibration.

It often seems natural to feel the feelings of those we are closest to. Like when a loved one is broken-hearted over a lost love, for example. We do it for a vast range of circumstantial experiences. However, in today's world, we are expanding our perceptions to feel the feelings of a broader range of people.

Some of the feelings that we have that we don't understand are perceptions of others feelings, or feelings associated with community or global circumstances. That's because the energy of the world is changing; it's more expansive. We are sensing our Oneness of Spirit. Furthermore, we are deepening our perceptions according to our increased personal growth. We also have a greater awareness of our unity and how we entertain the movement of energy as feelings through our bodies and interpret them in our minds.

We are using our abilities to transmute the energy of feelings into higher vibrations of love. When we feel our own feelings, detach from identifying with them, view them as energy passing through us, and feed them with compassion, they change. The wisdom is released into our minds, and the energy is freed to use for our creative purposes. This is how we give compassion to ourselves. This is how we purify the energy we experience in our own space. This is how we process our emotions so that we can speak the truth with creative kindness.

When we empathize with others, we help to transmute their feelings with love and compassion and emanate those feelings back to the projector of those feelings, the person who they came from. We break the cycle of negative, or harmful energy momentum. By doing this consciously, we serve the other person whom we care about. We derive intrinsic value from this action—a natural good feeling of accomplishment that we feel deeply inside.

In addition, the more we use our Life energy for positive purposes with love, the more love and Life energy we receive. Good energy cycles back to us, as does the quality of any energy that we project in our expressions. We illuminate our beings. The exponential positive effects on our own being also render positive incoming energy when we need it!

We are changing the energy of the world by understanding how we affect the quality of the energy that passes through our being. We use the "observer effect" phenomenon where the intention of the scientist affects the outcome of the experiment. Through pure intentions we can create positive feelings and positive thoughts. Positive thoughts create after their kind. The higher vibration invites inspired ideas. Positive feelings generate substance to form inspired ideas.

Whenever anybody faces challenges that upset their emotions, we are taking conscious action. We are pouring compassion into this energy to heal, purify, and transform it. Then we are attaching the purified energy to ideas of their intended reality that they wish to experience. We are using alchemy.

We are helping each other to realize and live our deepest desires as manifested experience. We now understand how to use the physics of energy within our bodies. Understanding the science of Spirit, we master our Life energy. The process becomes natural after practice, as do all of our applications of truth over time. As we unite, our power to manifest intensifies exponentially. As we realize the powers within, and unite in consciousness, we are taking energetic action to change our world for the better. We are building momentum to heal our entire planet and all of humanity of all sacrifice and suffering.

Because we are consciously raising the vibration of our Life energy to the level of compassion as we live our daily lives, our consciously created reality renders a higher quality of life on our planet. Life is becoming easier as we work with our Life energy of consciousness. We are helping others and being helped so much more! Compassion rules in our New World!

We are free to transform energy from what doesn't work in our world, and create our New World with the energy of compassion.

Brotherhood

When we truly realize our spiritual connection
during our cooperative endeavor to evolve along life's journey,
we sense the reality of our brotherhood; we appreciate very soul,
every relationship, every gift of Life.

Genuine appreciation expressed nourishes our soul...it is priceless.

Nurturing Souls with Appreciation

The rivers of Divinity
Seep out
In a loving touch
A moment of compassion
A helping hand

A tender touch
Pleasing aromas
Savory flavorful tastes
Love expressed
In a smile

Recognition of Godliness
Appreciation acknowledges
And satisfies deeply a soul
Noticing love's subtle expressions
With words of heartfelt confession
Illuminate our soul's inner glow

Visions of beauty
A kind word or deed
Any delightful sense
Deserves its reward
In simple acknowledgement

Our own soul
Blossoms in the
Garden of love
Whether we receive or
Express appreciation

Recognition of Godliness
Appreciation acknowledges
And satisfies deeply a soul
Noticing love's subtle expressions
With words of heartfelt confession
Illuminate our soul's inner glow

Whether stranger or friend
Or intimate partner
Siblings or children
Grandparents or Self
Notice God's love shining through

Nurture our souls
With gratitude often
Don't let good things
Go unspoken
Lift a spirit

Recognition of Godliness
Appreciation acknowledges
And satisfies deeply a soul
Noticing love's subtle expressions
With words of heartfelt confession
Illuminate our soul's inner glow

Recognizing God in All

We can feel and express the spirit of Brotherhood when we realize that every human on this planet that is alive has God in them, for God is Life. Some shine their goodness radiantly. Others may seem dim. Some may seem to live to benefit all with their good will; yet others may ignorantly express discordant or destructive energy. We all have the light of God to some degree. The more we focus our attention on the good in all, the brighter each one becomes. Whatever we give our attention to, we are helping to expand by directing our energy in that direction.

Every soul thrives on genuine appreciation. We are turning up the light in our world by expressing it sincerely from our hearts. Let's express it often.

When disturbing energy is emanated, it takes some extra effort to seek the good in a soul, but it is there. It's a hungry soul seeking the light the best way it knows how. Instead of blame, or judgment, take the higher road. Apply good will towards all and find something to appreciate in those that attempt to disturb our peace. Maintain peace and express appreciation. This is how we are changing the world.

As we express appreciation through kind words, or acts, or gifts from the heart, we nourish each other's soul. Appreciation is delicious soul food that helps us to grow in our light. As our Light expands, the more deeply we sense our brotherhood and love that we abide in. As we use our Life energy to express appreciation, we are Lighting the world.

With our persistent vigilance toward an expanded understanding of life, we are opening to our true heritage as brothers and sisters. Throughout the years, we have experienced both friend and foe, joys and disappointments, accomplishments and discouragement. All of the players in our lives have shown up on our stage with a particular Divine gift to offer in our evolution. In the end, we all discover our gifts, and whether a person or circumstance was considered negative or positive, we get to the end of the process with a feeling of appreciation for all.

Now that we are self-aware and extracting the lessons and meaning from our experiences and relationships consciously, we realize at the highest level of perspective, we truly are helping each other. Sometimes we experience lack of consideration or kindness; sometimes we feel we have been the whipping board of physical or verbal abuse. We have learned to stand in our integrity, act out of self-love, and change or sever relationships that cross our boundaries. The perpetrators are not our enemies. They stepped in to give us a lesson about setting boundaries, about knowing our intrinsic self-worth, independent of any outside need for approval. These are soul friends who are growing, helping us to grow, and who we are helping to grow as well. These are our brothers and sisters.

When we see political leaders, bosses at work, or religious leaders acting with less than full integrity, we are disappointed for the lack of adherence to the highest standards of conduct. They irritate us with actions that affect so many in a destructive way. They irritate us when they say one thing and do another. They all have a spark of God, or they wouldn't even be alive. These are our brothers and sisters.

When we pull our attention away from the destructive words and actions (and effects) and focus on their good aspects (whether consciously known or not), we serve the Light with our attention. We withdraw our personal energy from problems and causes and blaming; we re-direct our attention toward goodness, solutions, and find ways to make a positive difference. But we appreciate them for the awareness they bring. We allow them to walk their own path of evolution while drawing boundaries around what we stand for.

Now we are focusing our loving attention on positive actions of speaking out and uniting to dissolve challenges and implement solutions according to our personal passions. We are empowered to make a difference. However, let's focus on the good in each and every individual while demanding the truth and the restoration of integrity in our governments, commerce, and educational and religious institutions.

It's not so hard to love those who treat us well, even though there are still minor blips or wrinkles to iron out. We still draw our boundaries and express our authentic feelings. Mostly, though, we are experiencing deeper and deeper personally fulfilling relationships. We are all experiencing a common energy of loving cooperation, a sense of brotherhood that has expanded outside our family and friends.

Strength of unity in community is emerging. We are networking communities to feel the brotherhood of all humanity. We are supporting each other and the work that we came here to do in regards to personal and global transformation.

In our personal lives, people are there for us—people who are discovering and expressing their True Self—an expression of their unique Divinity. As we pay loving attention to the good in each soul that is emerging and expressing, we are illuminating God's light. We are uniting in Brotherhood. When we give and receive an abundance of appreciation to our Brothers and Sisters, we have the most valuable wealth of all.

Nature

Mommy Nature nurtures our inner child,
cleanses our soul, and refreshes our energy.
I just love Mommy Earth!

Green Healing

Feeling heavy energy
Chaos dwells inside of me
Stopping time just to be
Only green is what I see

Mother Nature, my reliable cure
Absorbing energy that is pure
Getting centered, being sure
Nothing more now to endure

Chakra demons blockage cease
Wheels of life get prana grease
Spiritual energy lends new lease
Deeply feeling inner peace

Love connects me to the whole
Bond with God sensed in my soul
Being present to console
Guidance comes about my role

New perspective totally
"What is" is perfect, now I see
God's love is always a part of me
Creating a new reality

Nurturing Nature

Imagine walking along the perfumed pathway of a beautiful brilliant multi-colored flower garden. Or imagine walking on a beach, or through a forest, or in the mountains. Imagine all the places in nature that you love. The essence of that energy soothes our very soul. It refreshes us. We are One with Nature, for our Life energy is God, and God is all life. We partake of each other's energy, among humanity and in Nature, in every breath we take. There are so many beautiful places in nature to just go and walk or sit and meditate or just marvel in its beauty.

Just think of how our Earth sustains us with food and resources that we count on to live. Somehow we got out of harmony with our Earth home. We saw it as our planet of habitation rather than as a living organism of which we are a part. We ignorantly have been destroying ourselves by taking part or allowing depletion and disintegration. Now we are restoring the harmony between humanity and our planet of habitation.

In our New World we are waking up to our stewardship of our beautiful and generous Mother Earth. We used to take Her resources for granted and use and abuse her. We depleted and destroyed natural resources through industry and commerce. We wasted a lot. We weren't aware of our own actions or the actions of others. But now we are learning the truth. We are becoming aware through Internet communication, green activists and groups, and balancing media equality, that our environment has been in grave danger.

Education of the masses is bringing to the forefront our awareness of the real brevity of the situation. No longer are the effects of environmental neglect and abuse hidden from the masses by the programming of selected ideas and values by the few who tried to dominate control over the media.

We are aware. We are learning what we can do individually and collectively to take continuous positive action to right our wrongs and restore our Earth to its natural pristine condition. We are part of Mother Earth.

We are voicing our intent to protect our natural environment, the homes of all creatures, and the harmony of all on Earth. We are willing to become aware of what we can each do personally and professionally to make a difference.

Love is the energy that transforms in every case. We are using our loving energy to educate, gain awareness, take positive action, make changes, and support the loving visions of solutions. We are implementing these solutions. We are using our Love energy directly to transform pollution. We are using less, recycling more, and abstaining from products and practices that damage our environment. We are actively supporting laws that prevent further degradation.

We love, adore, and appreciate Mother Earth. We are taking responsibility as stewards of all in our care that is Nature. We are nurturing our flowers, plants, trees, and all vegetation and land. We are nurturing and loving our animals, protecting their environments, and caring for the God of life within them. We are directing our love into the Earth consciously to transform the energy back into a state of perfection.

We are part of Mother Earth. The elements of Mother Earth are the same elements we are made of. We constantly exchange energies with our Planet Earth. What we do to her, we do to ourselves. Let's love her more.

We are aware, and we are increasingly creating more health and harmony between our nature and the nature of our planetary home. In our New World we are stepping up to the plate and living in harmony with the Essential Nature of our Earth mother.

Healing

The nurturing energy of Mother Nature herself
blesses us with unconditional healing.

Feeling Your Healing

Feel God's love
Within your heart
To feel your healing
Here's the start

Love heals all
As we all know
Feeling first
Then allowing its flow

Heart of love
Open wide
Allow love's flow
To come inside

Love from friends
Who hear you speak
Helps to serve
The Self you tweak

They understand
Promoting healing
Guiding you with
Love they're feeling

Love from family
With their care
Assures you that
They'll always share

Healing thoughts
That no longer serve
Experience the abundance
That we all deserve

Healing hearts
From deepest pain
Thankful for the
Lessons gained

Participating in
Love's cooperation
Unites our souls
And every nation

Healing of the Whole

The accelerated advancement of our personal being, although somewhat challenging at times, to say the least, is providing all of humanity the conditions to heal. We have been changing on the inside, each one of us. We may change at different rates, or in different ways, but there is an underlying essential evolving nature that is the same for all of us. We feel it in our hearts.

Each individual uses free will to make choices—choices that greatly affect the whole of humanity and our planet. More and more of us are attuning to the whole, raising our level of awareness of our true unity and personal Divinity, and using that awareness. This is breeding a spirit of cooperation. We are using the energy of Life at its highest vibrations because we care. We enjoy helping each other. We are doing more and more things together in expanding networks. Even in the same fields, people are openly sharing ideas and methods that work.

Healing is about adjusting to a new level of awareness and applying truth in our daily lives to become whole beings, realizing our highest potential.

Healing is occurring on all levels: physical, mental, emotional, spiritual, perceptual, political, and environmental. Our relationships are based on open communication and truth.

As truth provides awareness of undesirable circumstances, such as the risk of environmental catastrophes, we are finding our passion within and using our anger constructively to draw boundaries and stop destruction. We are now directing our energy into positive solutions. We are taking a stand for what we feel is right. Once aware, rather than channeling our energies toward the problem, we are co-creating solutions and channeling our energy into that direction with a clear vision of what we wish to accomplish in the end. We see clearly a clean, harmonious planet in our minds. We discover our purpose, and in addition, we do what we can each moment as we live along in life.

We have been sharing awareness in person, on the Internet, and more and more conscious intentions and solutions are being presented in all types of media.

We are healing from within each individual, throughout our lives and relationships, uniting as a whole team, and healing our whole planet. We are balancing the male and female energies within ourselves, on our planet, and throughout existence. This is our process. This is our service as we are evolving into a race that cares.

Our compassion for ourselves, and each other, is the energy we are using to heal. It truly is the highest form of love that casts aside outer appearances and does what's good, what is needed, what is required in the moment for Life.

Through awareness and compassion, we are finding balance as we raise our vibrations to higher expressions of love. We are realizing fighting, competition, or resistance is futile. Only love works. Only love heals. Love is our solution. It is the only energy that can change other energy. By using the alchemy of love, we are healing ourselves, each other, and our planet.

All Life is energy. Conscious energy. Since energy cannot be created nor destroyed, we can only change its form—through love. Consciousness is awareness and love. We are healing by purifying and transforming the energy of our world into its natural state.

We are becoming whole individually as we master our personal energy, and we are becoming whole globally as we unite with our common feelings and shared purpose.

By using the energy of love, which is innately unifying, we are healing our Whole Self and our Whole Planet.

It **is** a New World After All, isn't it?

Presence

Presence is the key to freedom, so you can only be free now.

Eckert Tolle
Practicing The Power of Now

Time is Now

There is no time but now
But time goes by somehow
My memories tell me of a past
My present never seems to last
Precious moments strung through time
Create this current life of mine

Life is time...Time is now
I'm going to make it count somehow

The me I was before is gone
My future sings a brand new song
Since I create my life anew
I decide to make my dreams come true
Now all my desires, hopes, and dreams
Are finally coming true for me

Life is time...Time is now
I'm going to make it count somehow

Fulfilling my soul purpose is now my career
Right livelihood is my experience here
Relationships heal and grow through love
Close bonds exist that were never dreamed of
From deep inside comes my inspiration
Life fulfills all of my aspirations

Life is time...Time is now
I'm going to make it count somehow

It's not just me — it's all of us
We're standing on a precipice
In this New Year especially
Let's create the world the way we know it could be
Our expanded awareness to another dimension
Will light the world with our conscious intention

Life is time...Time is now
We're going to make it count somehow

Now our lives are demonstrated spiritually
Kindness prevails eternally
We will lovingly care for our Mother Earth
So she may never cease giving birth
Our love heals humanity forevermore
No more hunger, greed, hate, or war

Life is time...Time is now
We're going to make it count somehow

The Precious Moment

We experience the flow of Life as we exist in each moment of now. Every moment is a gift—a valuable gift of Life. As we recognize the gifts in each moment, we realize how precious Life is; both our gratitude and awareness expand. We gain the highest value out of life when we are fully present with our attention on each person, place, or aspect within each moment. As we tune in, we sense the flow of Love.

We have the gift of abundant Life energy from God, our Source, and the opportunity to direct it according to our free will. We have the freedom to choose our thoughts and feelings in each moment. We simultaneously interpret and create our experiences in each now moment.

We can experience our outer reality with deep appreciation. We can see "what is" and feel "what is." Acceptance of "what is" puts us into our Center where we are free to create in each now moment. Our experiences in Life range from loving moments with intimate partners, affection with family and friends, breathing in the essence of Nature, laughing and celebrating at parties to crying for our losses, or even to mundane things like cleaning the house.

We are increasing our attention to, and depth of, inner experiences these days. We are tuning in to the presence of God as we listen to the still, small voice within. As we listen to Divine guidance, we gain awareness of ourselves and we consciously choose to improve. Inside, we integrate our experiences with our expanded perception and become wiser. Our very Eternal Self blossoms into our outer personality. We benefit immensely from these changes by raising the quality of our Life with our essence, or Being.

To reconcile the truth that Life is change, and still stop to "be" in the now moment, helps us to understand our focal point of consciousness and how we fit into and harmonize with the whole. We are aware of our True Self and our eternal nature. We are aware of God, our unlimited Source of Life. This is where we catch the wave of Life and surf to its crest with expanded awareness. This is where we access and feel the love that is all-inclusive. We all bond in this place energetically. Here is where we are open to receive all of the good things Life has to offer.

We used to hurry so fast. We used to be so caught up in the "rat race" that we almost went into full rote living, hardly having time to pay attention to our feelings or passions. We thought we had to do that to survive. We thought, "That's the way it is." But now that we know that just isn't true, we are slowing down, and "being" in each precious moment. AND we are consciously creating more than we ever had before! We are mastering our energies, transforming them with love, and creating more loving, peaceful, and joyful experiences.

In this New World, we are truly beginning to live up to our name: we are humans "being," and we are being more joyously and abundantly alive than ever before in each precious moment!

Intention

"Before you tell your life what you intend to do with it,
listen for what it intends to do with you."

Parker J. Palmer

Modeling Life

Consciousness is the clay, or Source of what we make
Our intentions give directions for the forms to take
The love in our hearts is the energy
The essence in motion that stops to be

Our consciousness is the light we turn into form
The ideas of our mind will all be born
If we are not aware of how we create
We still experience the forms of our mistake

Our supra-consciousness is ultimately in control
If we're not alert our foibles take their toll
All levels of consciousness come into play
In the end all is perfect, come what may

All practice is valuable to what we are learning
But conscious creators are no longer yearning
They observe and take control of their mind
Ideas blend with love, these people are kind

By being aware of how we create
We love ourselves and others with dreams that we make
Conscious of life and how we're evolving
No longer perplexed by the problems we're solving

But now we are all conscious and using
All data from life that's no longer confusing
The recipe for reality and absolving all pain
Has its basis in love from which we all gain

Suddenly, as we unite, we heal all of humanity
We suffer no more from separateness or vanity
With cooperation we live in joy and peace
The healing comes from the love we increase

Intentional Living

Now that we know we are creating our lives and our world, and every experience we have, we are consciously setting intentions. Intentions are statements of what we wish to create or experience. It's an awareness of where to place our Life energy via our attention, or consciousness director.

We are fertilizing our intention seeds for manifestation with the energy momentum of our attention. We "think" on purpose. We carefully choose our words as we "speak" on purpose. We "feel" emotional feelings that we choose, or transmute with love, and direct that energy into our intentions. We take action toward the fulfillment of each intention that is in alignment with our Divine Purpose.

Our lives are laced with Purpose. We are gaining more clarity than ever before about what life is about and what we are up to. Individually, we have identified our talents and passions and we use our unique abilities to make a positive difference to those whose lives we touch. As we discover our purpose, individually and globally, we have the basis for setting conscious intentions that are in alignment with the whole. We are aware of our individual part in the Divine Plan for Peace on Earth. We maximize our energy efficiency by using Purpose as our motivational force.

We tell the truth on Purpose because truth connects us to the whole. Even when the truth may hurt, we stand in our own integrity on behalf of the virtue of Honesty. We tell the truth with compassion, and surround difficult truisms with sincere compliments. We serve awareness. We serve each other by intentionally being truthful and authentic.

Our level of self-awareness and self-control has granted us the blessings of awakened beings. What happens is what we intend to happen as we co-create within the infrastructure of the Divine Plan.

Individually, our intentions set the energy to attract people, circumstances, and resources that resonate with our talents, interests, and goals. We are magnetizing like energies like never before. Our lives are getting easier and easier as a result.

When we find ourselves tapping into the depth of our being, we are tuned in to our souls and connection to the whole, and we set high-level intentions. Our lives change rapidly when we grow into our intentions gleaned from higher levels of awareness. We are changed forever, and for the better. There's no going back.

We are discovering and using the principles of unified group intentions. We are synergizing our consciousness in group settings, and virtually—in real time, to provide maximum beneficial results toward positive solutions that are good for one and all. We are co-creating myriad forms of win-win situations in our business and personal affairs. We are using the new powerful energy of peaceful cooperation that has replaced force and competition.

We are literally putting our minds together and making life better in all ways. We are making ourselves better rapidly with our conscious intentions in terms of our beingness of who we are and how we show up.

As we become aware of what doesn't work in our world, solutions emerge. We are shifting quickly into our new level of awareness. We are sharing processes of obtaining awareness with each other, and we are healing energy blockages with the alchemy of love.

We are now living our lives with full awareness of our Unity and setting conscious intentions for a Purposeful lifestyle. As we move into our Unity of Purpose, we are co-creating our New World as a place of peace and harmony, abundance and joy, understanding and compassion.

This New World is more "real" than in the past because we intentionally live the Truth.

Attention

By the conscious direction
of our attention
toward pure intentions...

we master our lives.

Consciously Creating Reality

When humans understand how love transforms
Distorted perceptions are no more
The reality we create as experience on earth
Will render peace and harmony as we yield the birth

Of what we imagine and feel inside
From perceived suffering when true self hides
To consciously creating in the flow of life's love
Experiencing exactly what our dreams are made of

In the stillness and silence where we reach our core
Our expansive awareness feeds illusion no more
The voice of our soul sends out through our feelings
The wisdom of mastery of life and its dealings

Drawing wisdom from feelings we now clearly see
How to use the physics of oneness that new senses perceive
Transforming all energies with love's intention
Using consciousness wisely, directing our attention

Attention now reserved for the ideas we choose to form
Into physical reality, mistakes no longer born
Harnessing energy from which all is created
With love we create the peace long awaited

As we accept the darkness and love it as well
We melt all with the light as wisdom will tell
The transformation of energy to what we enjoy
Renders feelings of delight and life is our toy

No longer wrestling or resisting outer reality
Expressions of love form our personality
While love transforms in our individual space
It becomes the energy of the world in every case

We are now awake with awareness of all
And how Self fits in answering Life's call
We shine our own light as we hone who we are
Increasing our luminosity as a bright love star

Conscious Creation

We are sending energy to whatever we give our attention to. Our personal Life energy is our bank account of light and love. Our consciousness is light and love. Conscious energy flows through our mind. Feelings emanate from our soul through our heart. Together they make up our personal energy system.

Our consciousness is directed by our thoughts, and the energy of our emotions follows suit. Our emotions are energy in motion and it manifests form with the light of our mind into our reality. It's pure physics.

When we give any one or any thing our attention, we are "paying" our energy as we "pay attention." When we direct our energy with thoughts and emotions, we form reality. We create the life that we live.

The ideas we entertain in our mind create the form of physical reality. This light forms the emotional energy in our space into the experiences of our life. It also has an effect on the world. We deliver our energy into the collective consciousness where thoughts can be received by others. Ideas build momentum when many people deliver their energy to them. Where do you think all your thoughts come from? Where do you think your thoughts go?

Thoughts inspired by Divinity through our soul and mind, deliver a feeling of exhilaration. When we tune in to them and follow the guidance of our soul, we find our personal passion and our unique expression. Personal expression of creative energy, backed by individual purpose, extends a wealth of joy and enlivens life. The Divine connection is mastered by allowing love's flow to be directed by conscious thought. Conscious thought is derived through expanded awareness through our hearts.

When we aren't aware that we are creating our experiences, it is because there is so much time between the time we imagine and the time we experience the reality. Also it has not been part of our belief system to picture something and then experience it. Since purposeful creation of reality didn't exist in our realm possibility, we weren't even expecting or alert to common synchronicity. We had not been using our creative powers consciously. Until now.

We've noticed how commercials and news reports and various forms of media have "captured" our attention. Was our energy given freely? Yes. Was it given with the consciousness of a psychic observer?

The psychic observer watches information that is paid attention to with the awareness of the motive behind the information and the essence of what the information is creating. For example, commercials are overtly trying to sell something as well as the mindset to go with it. However, each media production has a motive and uses the attention of the audience to build its essence into form. Some news stations have reportedly used sensationalism to dramatize the news, instead of delivering unbiased raw facts, reflecting impure motives. Information that the public "should" buy into comes through various agencies, companies, or institutions. We might wonder what the government wants us to think according to what is presented.

When we learn to apply the wisdom of the Beatles song, "Let It Be," and turn our attention away from what we don't want to create into an experience, event, or global condition, we will no longer give it the energy that allows it's existence. Negative, anti- ("against" anything), or fear energy is energy all the same.

By creating a target of conscious intentions of what we do want to create, we manifest them more quickly and successfully with the focus of our energy. We direct our consciousness by visioning, or imagining, our desired result. As we fill in the details with our imagination through conscious dreaming, or directed imagination, the injection of strong emotions sets the energy of our reality before us. In fact, when we develop faith and positive expectation, we nurture our imagined inventions. Consistent fertilization with our thoughts and beliefs strengthens our exercised power of co-creation with God. The more emotional charge we put into it, the faster and more secure the manifestation.

We are becoming masters of our Life Energy. In our awakening process, we are consciously choosing our intentions that support our desires and life purpose, what we want to create for our outer experiences, and consciously directing our attention, solely focused on our purpose. We are mastering our lives by mastering the conscious direction of our attention. We are acutely aware now, that what we put our attention on, we create. Each and every moment we ask ourselves: "Is what I'm thinking about or looking at or somehow taking into my psyche what I want to create?" Faster and faster, we are using a new level of awareness to self-govern our thoughts, and thus our lives, until we are consistent with the conscious use of our attention. Our Life Energy is now completely reserved for what we truly wish to create as our experience.

While realizing our connection to the whole, we elicit our intentions from our souls so that we know they are what fits into the Divine Plan. In our still, quiet moments that we have created by stopping the action frenzy of our old life patterns, clarity has emerged.

Once totally connected to our Eternal Self through acceptance and recognition of our feelings, we accept our true heart's desires as our birthright. Now we envision the experience of those desires in our minds, knowing full well that we are creating. We fill these thought forms with love from deep within our hearts. We feel the joy in the now moment as we create our images and give thanks. We relish our freedom to create our lives and our world.

When we are consciously in a visioning process, we check our thoughts continually to assure alignment with our purpose and intentions. We align our will with God's will and hold the vision with the surrender to God so that we can be assured our creation is good for one and all. While we co-create with God in this way, our actual manifested experiences turn out to be better than what we could have ever imagined on our own.

Individually, we have become vigilant in our conscious direction of our thoughts, feelings, words, and actions. We are vigilant in the processing of our feelings, speaking our truth, and harnessing the energy of our emotions and directing that energy into our conscious intentions. We have changed dramatically. We feel better and life is easier.

We are supporting each other to realize our dreams as we gather in groups and use processes of Conscious Creation. By using synergized group consciousness (uniting our hearts and minds and focusing on single united intentions), we feel the power of uniting in love, and the effects of such processes are permanently changing our consciousness and our lives. We are using the law of energy momentum and attraction to quickly access physical (material), mental (clarity and receptivity), and spiritual desires. We are manifesting miracles!

Many cooperative group endeavors are producing astonishing results toward positive global changes. We are using conference forums, retreat spaces, and the internet to connect and unite our conscious intentions. We are taking action together as we encourage and help one another. Our actions are initiated by placing group attention on positive solutions.

We are now using the power of our attention to create our world of peace, freedom, and abundance. We are living lives of joy in a united brotherhood, weaving our dream ideas into physical reality.

We have created a New World. The idea seeds have been planted, and our harvest time has come. We are a world of Conscious Creators.

The guidance of Divinity insures harmony as we each attune our inner Consciousness Director with God, our Divine Director. Natural cooperation ensues. It is this cooperation that is the key to the peace that we seek. In our minds and hearts Peace is here now.

Choice

A choice of pure intent,
holding the space for goodwill toward all,
allows peace and harmony
to exist undisturbed.

Love or Fear

When you think for a moment it's really quite clear
We can come from love or we can come from fear
It all sounds so simple to make the best choice
When we come from love our souls rejoice

Simple love flows purely from our heart
With infinite variety of expression to impart
We can smile, lend a hand, give a kiss or a hug
We can wrestle and play, roll around on the rug

We can love ourselves, too, as we play
We could laugh and sing or stay in nature all day
We could take a bath with candles afire
We could dream of having our heart's desire

But fear, it's more tricky, we don't always discern
How to make the best choice, but we can learn
Reactions are habits that can come from fear
Our anger or resistance affects those that are near

Judgment is fear of what we don't accept
Feeling this energy many have wept
Jealousy is fear of not being special enough
Losing your love mate would be really tough

Fear of anything sends your attention to it
It attracts it right to you with energy conduit
We know we send energy with our attention
With every thought or word that we mention

Now we are learning and changing fast
Fear is becoming a thing of the past
With love from our hearts we make each decision
Love's arrow creates joy with certain precision

Spiral Towards the Light

We are each either spiraling toward the light, or descending toward the darkness, depending on our choices.

All of our behavioral choices are based either in love or in fear. Our behavior, or beingness, consists of our beliefs, thoughts, words, actions, and expectations. They form the realm of our experience according to the sum total of their vibrations and our personal intentions.

Our values center around what we believe. If we value love and kindness, then we have beliefs about how we should behave, or work towards, with consideration toward others. If we value money and power, then we behave and work towards being rich and having a high status in the world's terms. People who value money and power above love are living an illusion of fear; either superiority or that there's not enough for all.

Those who value and express love are rich because the light of their being is attractive and their virtues find expression. This creative flow of unique love is what attracts abundance in the new energy of the world.

The bottom line of defining self and personal expression is what is valued and intended. It is usually evident by the way a person treats others. An awareness of True Self is imperative in the energy of our New World. We know we are love at our core. It's where we derive self-worth and creative inspiration to propel us toward the light as we make choices in our daily lives.

Love-based decisions propel us toward our highest good, towards the light, and our most beneficially enjoyable experiences of life. They help us reach our goals of personal evolution, too. Choosing to come from love each time sounds so simple.

It is simple, but it's not always easy, is it?

Jesus told us to love others as ourselves. Have your ever loved anyone more than yourself, gave up being true to yourself to keep their love or to make them happy, and then resented yourself or them for it? We can get into some pretty sticky wickets if we're not careful.

Have you ever lost sight of consideration for another and simply acted out of pure self-interest, then hurt somebody you loved and deeply regretted it? Sometimes choices like these can change the course of our lives.

Not all choices provide such extreme outcomes, but every choice counts for something. It speaks of who we are and what we stand for. Whether we are loving our self or loving others, if we practice accessing love from God, our Source, and set the intention to come from love, we can grow into a more loving life. Everyone will benefit from who we are. After all, expressing the love that we are is natural.

However, fear is natural for us, too. At least it seems to be in our awakening state when we are not completely free of illusion. In the land of duality and illusion, things are not what they seem, but what they seem may cause us to react in fear.

Judgment is a form of fear. When we judge others, for some reason, we feel like they are a threat to our personal happiness if they don't live according to the beliefs that we are convicted to. Just take a look at that word, convicted. Are you a convict, a prisoner of your own beliefs?

In our New World we are choosing our beliefs. We are learning that although there is Universal Truth and Universal Law that we abide by, or face the consequences, within that broad realm we are open to infinite possibilities. Accepting and loving others opens us up to a broader range of possibilities and gives them the freedom to live by God's design. You are responsible for your choices, and they are responsible for theirs, but we are not here to judge each other. We just keep choosing love, for our Self, and for others, equally.

Negative anger is the fear of experiencing our own pain. We avoid pain and store it within us until someone pushes our buttons. We have the choice of lashing out at them, or being with our pain in private until we get the awareness out of it. By internal processing we can resolve our inner issues. After this process, the feeling of anger evolves to appreciation for healing this energy blockage.

Positive anger is the fear of someone overstepping our boundaries. Again, we can react or choose to take a look at what boundary issues are coming up. Then we can express those boundaries with compassionate, yet firm, communication.

We can choose to change the energy in the room by our countenance. We set our energy field by our expectations: positive expectations yield positive results and negative expectations yield negative results.

Ultimately, we are up against ourselves. We choose our beliefs and our values. We choose our thoughts, words, and actions. We choose our expectations. We get the quality of energy back that we have put out. Our experiences are our own creations of personal energy.

We decide who we are, how we treat others, and what we stand for. Just like you can tell a tree by its fruit, you can tell the level of integrity of a person by their outward expressions—how they live.

Remember, every single choice is important. Choose love. It's the only energy that works in our New World.

Balance

Conscious awareness of "what is"
combined with adjustments from lessons learned
blends to form a new awareness
where balance is naturally restored.

Equilibrium

Balance aspects of each whole
Stay on track to reach the goal
Spirit, body, heart, and mind
Never leaving one behind

Emotion alone leaves logic behind
Intelligent choice employs the mind
Sense the truth the heart's revealing
Balance reason with the feeling

Too much work wears one out
Listen to the body shout
Play, sing, dance, have fun
Be sure to rest when you are done

Play that never ends sounds great
But your life's purpose cannot wait
Creative work is fun besides
Balance energy on both sides

Make time for people to show you care
Enjoy relationships as you share
Spend time alone to listen inside
Feel your heart opening wide

Expressing energy from inner core
To outside world will yield some more
Balancing inner and outer endeavor
Produces a soul that's ingeniously clever

Meditation opens Heaven's Gate
Experience grounds each personal trait
Relationships, career, personality, health
Balanced whole brings personal wealth

Equilibrium achieved by balancing act
Propels one forward to be exact
On course of life which one aspires
Successfully achieving soul desires

Balanced Living

In our process of attaining Self-Mastery, we are balancing and uniting all aspects of ourselves and our lives. Internally, we are balancing our male and female energies, our mind and our hearts, our thoughts and our feelings, and our spirit and our body. Externally, we are balancing and bringing into harmony our relationships, our career, our physical health, and our personality traits. We are unifying our inner and outer worlds as we replace egoic perceptions of separation with the realization of Oneness that we have come to know in our hearts.

In our process of becoming whole, we have created intense experiences of conflict and change, to the point where we want nothing but peace. We are drawn within to find Inner Peace. We are standing our ground to eliminate facets of our lives that disrupt our peace. Our hearts are guiding us to listen to our feelings.

We are finding our authentic selves and being present with each other as we grow together. This period of rapid transformation is about balance.

Our goals and intentions that lead to self-mastery consist of focused energy toward fulfilling relationships with people that match our energy vibrations, directing our careers toward our heart's passions, letting go of addictions and destructive beliefs around health while treating our bodies well, and expressing the unique virtues and talents that we have come to know are our essence. We are extending ourselves to care about our fellow humans and our environment.

We have been multi-tasking in personal transformation, and we have made great progress!

Individually, we discover and master ourselves, and then find our part in the Divine Plan to serve others. We are living according to internal clues and intuition rather than exterior circumstances. As we drop the victim perspective and take responsibility for our lives, we are mastering our balanced energy with wise choices.

Globally, we are trading in materialistic values for a more spiritual value system based on caring and sharing. This balance is happening in a forced way for some, but it is conscious choice on the part of many. We trade, cooperate, and extend ourselves to help each other. We lift each other up as we bring our lives into balance.

In our relationships, we have called people into our lives that we energetically balance with through the energy exchange of relating. We have discovered hidden parts of us, including shadows. We bring them into the light and transform our very beings.

In our careers, we have quit the rat race and put materialistic values aside to live a more simple and fulfilling life while pursuing our dream occupations. We are balancing time spent on careers with time spent on other areas of our lives, such as personal relationships, personal development, and body care.

While balancing all aspects of our lives, we are being present with our own essence. We are integrating our inner aspects into our outer personality. Moment to moment we live attuned to the feelings of ourselves and others. We listen deeply. We express ourselves as we come into balance. We perceive truth, and live it.

We are growing in our awareness of truth. We are turning truth awareness into wisdom by our daily thoughts, words, and actions. We are walking our talk.

The balancing that we have done has helped to create a world of harmony. Our New World is balanced and whole.

Attunement

Attunement is conscious connection to the whole.
It is where we fall into lockstep with life
and experience the freedom to be.

The Geometry of Love

Square   +   Circle   =   Love Heart

Male   Female   Inner Child

Love's mystery is found in sacred geometry
A universal language that can set us free
The duality illusion is just a game that we play
It's fun, but remember there is another way

Although we see both dark and light
We live by day; we sleep by night
While there is both short and tall
There's something the same about it all

Notice all is glued by love that is bonding
Pulsing through our hearts, our life is responding
This is the energy that creates physical reality
Love is the essence of all causality

You can sense it inside, that's where we feel it
But now there's more, let me reveal it
The circle halved upon the square that's turned
Creates a heart symbol for the love that we yearn

We mix inside energies female and male
Our many lives balanced as we tell our tales
With the yin and yang of our inner world tied
We calibrate with God as wisdom is applied

The merger of opposites back into unity
Transforms into essence, innocence and purity
Inner strength grows, outer concerns become mild
We give new birth to our Inner Child

With this birth comes a new awareness
A stark realization piercing our bareness
In this place we are one with our Creator
Although we are humbled, we couldn't be greater

Unlimited love right from our Source
Shifted, we turn 90 degrees on our course
With duality reconciled we find our ascension
Consciousness moves to a higher dimension

Attunement of Self to Whole

We are all uniting in the true home in our hearts through Divine prompting and assistance. We are making the conscious choice to surrender our personal wills and attune with the Divine Intelligence that creates perfection in life. We are in harmony with Life as a result of our attunement. We are going with the flow!

The flow of Life, or consciousness, spirals through our being, and is the energy of who we are. When we calibrate our personal unit of consciousness to the whole of consciousness, we are able to express our Divinity and natural perfection. We know who we truly are and what we are up to in this lifetime.

Our personal and global shift in consciousness will be complete when enough people consciously attune to Divine Will. When the critical mass has been reached, the mass consciousness will naturally affect the minds of those who have not willingly participated in the Divine Plan.

As we accept our purpose to evolve, and begin to make conscious choices around unity consciousness, our world takes a giant leap toward global evolution. We are resolving conflicts by embracing paradoxes.

One such paradox is reflected in the area of math. The conflict in the realm of mathematics has been dual notions: one being "straight line math," or base 10, and the other being "curved line math," or base 12. In straight line math there are a series of connected points where there is no outside point to be in relation to. In curved line math, there are a series of points having relations to points outside the series. When the line is curved, both an interior and an exterior are evident.

The evolution of consciousness is mathematically described by Sacred Geometry. In sacred geometry there are both straight and curved lines. In our bodies we have both straight and curved lines of energy flow. Our spine is the straight line, and energy flows through our chakras in a curved, or spiral direction. By uniting these notions, we find the solutions to Life. We are thinking more in terms of both/and from the core of our hearts, instead of either/or from limiting beliefs around separation in our minds, to perceive truth more readily. Our minds and our hearts are joining forces to serve Life.

We are resolving our consciousness paradox by accepting our inner and outer worlds as both being real. We can see duality and separation when we look out into the world. When we place our attention within, we know our Oneness. We are balancing our inner and outer experiences. We stop to "be" and suddenly our lives shift dramatically for the better. Our inner worlds are expansive. As we realize the wealth within, we are experiencing wealth in our outer experiences as well. Through attunement, we become aware of our Divine purpose, our natural unique value, and the abundance of Life.

We are becoming aware of our energetic physiology by understanding our chakras and meridians, and internal energy flow. As we place our attention in our hearts, we open the door to other dimensions using our Christ Consciousness. We step into other dimensions. We feel our connections. We are united with the whole and access the genius of Universal Mind, and the Love of God.

We are clearing our energy blockages due to repressed feelings of the past. As we release and transmute the energy of our repressed feelings, we are gaining the revelations of our soul's wisdom. These are the "Revelations" spoken of in the Bible. We are discovering latent powers that we temporarily forgot when we held beliefs based on separation.

These "end times" are only the beginning of our peaceful New World. We are opening our hearts—to ourselves, to each other, and to God. We are attuning to the feelings in our hearts and increasing the flow of Love—the energy of Life. We are consciously creating using our abundance of Life energy derived by attuning to God, our Source of love in our hearts, and we are using the energy of Love constructively to create our Peaceful Paradise that was prophesied. Our sense of separation has lifted, we are united through attunement, we are whole, and we are happy in our New World.

Harmony

Peaceful cooperation
brings us to our greater experience
where we can enjoy the complete harmony
of life flowing naturally.

Peace of Heart

Compassion fills me
For whole of self
Two bodies, two lives
One soul
Two parts of the same whole

Attunement together
With Divine will
Brings peace of heart
Through understanding
And Divine love

For this I pray
Soothing, releasing
Comforting our hearts
That express Divine truth
Through two perspectives
Uniting together in God

Unconditional love
Deep devotion and caring
Lifetimes of sharing
And coming together
Through the essence
Of Pure love

Evolving, changing
Union so innocent
At once open, magnetic
Separate only for a moment
Unique callings
Pure love endures

Peace of heart
Pure Divine love
Supersedes all pain
Ever deeper, ever reuniting
Never ending
Thanks to God

Loving Cooperation

When we attune to Divine will, we each tune in through our Higher Self to our Source, God. We experience spiritual unity. As we realize our wholeness by attunement, we become clear about our purpose, our part in life, and how to relate to others. This brings much peace to our hearts.

Relationships can really be a challenge sometimes. There can be numerous differences between people due to diverse preferences, mindsets, personalities, levels of spiritual evolution, and varying values and perspectives. Although our differences are many, the place where we meet in relationship can be completely harmonious.

If we find ourselves in a discordant relationship with someone, we can pray for attunement to Divine will together and ask for clarity around the purpose of our relationship. This way, we can eliminate any extraneous undertakings that cause discord with the person, and work on the same goal together. We can each find our Divine place in the whole scheme of things. If both parties are in agreement, a joint prayer to attune to God's will and clarity around the purpose of the relationship can bring about miraculous insights and solutions.

When we are in tune with God, we are in tune with love. God is love. In the spirit of love, as we relate to others through our own loving essence, we just let them be who they are. Total acceptance. We don't need to tell them what to do and they don't need to tell us what to do. Sometimes we are inspired to share information or make suggestions, but we have no agenda for their lives. Each person is free to walk his or her own path.

As we pray for clarity around our own soul's purpose for this lifetime, we naturally begin to understand ourselves more and what we're here for. Just setting the intention to know our reason for living allows meaning to flow into our life. When attuned to Divine will, we realize not only our unique purpose, but also how to harmonize with every aspect of our lives.

When people are clear about their purpose and on their path, they realize their uniqueness lends a certain specialization. There is no feeling of competitive energy when one is really tuned in. Instead, souls who are clear about their life's mission seek each other out to cooperate. Everybody knows they're on the same team.

Our unique purpose is inspired by love. We are each inspired to love. As we relate and cooperate, we are finding it easy to keep it light because love is light. We laugh a lot, now, don't we? It's amazing how much more fun life is! We laugh when we make mistakes. We laugh at how we used to be. Whenever a situation begins to turn heavy or negativity seeps in—take a step back and laugh. Crack a joke or do something silly.

In our New World, we are uniting at the soul level. Whether it is in a personal or business relationship, we are finding it much easier to live in peace and harmony.

We are living in peaceful cooperation. It feels so good to relate with kind, compassionate, conscious people. Everybody is so nice and friendly and helpful. What a great New World we live in.

We are consciously aware that we are all working together for the benefit of the whole. We are the whole. We are one in the whole and the whole in one. We all cooperate in the spirit of love and everyone is a winner! Imagine that! Feel it deeply. Enjoy the experience inside and out.

Focus

With conscious use of constructive energy
and pure focus,
we can move mountains.

Laser Love

Expanded awareness
Possibilities all
Light forms
Love's call

Presence conscious
Eternally
Ever unfolding
Naturally

Powerful love
Character of Source
Alpha and omega
Surround life's course

Individuation
Comprises a soul
Conscious of Self
Aspect of whole

Looking out
Creates illusion
Of separation
Causing confusion

Source within
Creates without
Creator perspective
Removes all doubt

Laser beam of
Loving intention
Manifesting outwardly
Thought's invention

Wholeness awareness
We are one
Serve another
For Self it is done

Attention to the Divine Plan:
The Ultimate Vision

Part of the Divine plan is to become Self-aware. We have transformed our structure of reality to see that life works from the inside out, and not the other way around. As we work on the microcosm within ourselves, we have an effect on the macrocosm without energetically. We change the world by changing ourselves. After an intense period of personal transformation, we discover our hidden passions.

When we meditate, or listen inside, we perceive what goals are embedded in our souls. Our connection to the Divine ensures us that all is well. Inside we perceive the Divine plan and our place within it. We get detailed ideas and inner knowingness about the larger picture in Life—what is happening and why, as well as what next.

Once having perceived the Divine Plan, we focus our energy on personal, group, community, and global intentions that serve that Plan. We each have a critical part to play, and we are stepping up to the plate to fulfill our Divine Mission. We know our Personal Life Purpose through the passions of our hearts. We are tuning in to what we feel strongly about, what brings us joy. We are creating a new kind of life by following our passions.

Once having found our place and gaining enough clarity and resources to move forward with our mission, we begin our new career and then we network with others. We share our visions and our passions. We look for places where we can blend our talents and resources. We share what we know and what we have to be of help. We get a lot of help from others. We create in joy and gratitude in the spirit of loving cooperation.

We are finding our balance between energy spent on our individual part and in cooperating with others. Both individual and group efforts are necessary for the fulfillment of the Divine Plan. We create uniquely alone, and our self expression is satisfying. In the spirit of cooperation we share our creations and ideas. As we share our ideas, solutions, and processes, we form a myriad of synthesis creations, each one especially unique.

Within each of us, and together, we are making inroads to overturn the effects of past energy mis-creations in the form of negative earthly conditions and events. We are taking both inner and outer action as we heal each other and our planet to experience wholeness and harmony.

We are bonding our visions to see the Ultimate Vision of our personal and global transformation. As we realize the Divine Intent behind all of our visions, we fully understand the master plan and the result of our directed energy focus. And now, we are grounding this vision into the reality of our new life on earth— an awakened life.

The key to discovering the master Divine Plan is to continue to communicate and bond our visions. With our bonded vision, we can create an energy momentum so vast that the tide of Life will wash over our world like a tidal wave. The energy flow will sweep away unwanted debris and leave for us a world of cooperative love—world peace at last.

Now we keep aligning our attention with the Ultimate Vision of the Divine plan, perceive and play our part with our focused attention, and Life is flowing naturally into a state of perfect peace, harmony, and abundance.

We are co-creating with God. We are securing peace and harmony in our own lives. We will secure peace and harmony in the world through our focused cooperative visions and efforts.

It is already a New World—WE CAN SEE IT!

Success

Success is pure Essence expressed.

Success

Looking out
Makes you pout
When you see the world in fear

Looking in
Makes you win
When you feel the love so near

Delving inside
Creates inner pride
By expressing the real you

Magnitudinous success
Is achieving the best
Of what your soul has set out to do

Deep, deep down
Absorbing love found
Creates our inspiration

By being aware
Life doesn't scare
But becomes a celebration

Stop to be
Rest by a tree
Just relax and let life flow

Listen to feelings
It's wisdom revealing
The messages from your soul

Don't stop trying
There is no dying
Life is eternally renewing

Truth is knowing
Your soul is glowing
It's happy whatever you're doing

Success: New and Improved!

Remember not so very long ago, when we thought that money and status was the measure of success?

Rich people were considered powerful. Some used their method of money exchange for control over others. Many impoverished people were taken advantage of in sweat shops around the world. Many rich people found out that money doesn't buy love or happiness. Numerous poor people found out that the love and good times they shared was more valuable than anything money could buy.

Status, achieved by position or title, generated perceived superiority. A few examples of status positions would be an executive, a government official, a doctor or other professional with an educational degree. When accomplishment is accompanied by goodwill, it is of supreme benefit to our world. When perceived superiority or authority became a means to dominate or control, then it damages the self-esteem of others while robbing them of their freedom. Many of us didn't own our personal power—we shared this mentality—and we made a lot of choices based on this belief system. Now that we have chucked that belief system, freedom is back!

We laugh at the absurdity of these old values, as in the bumper sticker that says: "Whoever has the most toys when they die wins." We now realize that true power comes from love.

There's no judgment. We all pick our life circumstances to learn various lessons. It's great to have an abundance of money. In fact in our New World, we know we deserve it and can create it. However, we realize it's just a tool, one medium of exchange. It's not something we acquire through deception, force, or greed.

There's no failure. We are already successful. It's built into the very fabric of Life! All we have to do is look inside and express the essence of who we are. This brings satisfaction to our soul. We are now living from the inside out, instead of from the outside in. We now identify with the essence of our soul instead of our earthy role. We desire less from the outside because we are fulfilled from the inside. We are rich with inspiration, compassion, and understanding.

Success is expressing our own unique version of wisdom, creativity, and love. If somehow we get confused or our perception of Reality gets distorted, we can always get back on track by placing our attention inside to the core of our being—our guiding light. We just persevere and keep on trying. The irony is that trying denotes doing something, but really we're just "being" pure, and expressing ourselves naturally.

In our New World, we are masters of being. Our consciousness is now being directed by our soul. We are balanced and whole. We are successful as we re-create our inner world into a place of peace and total unconditional self-love.

When we expand our heaven within to the outside world through expression, we are truly living love "on earth as it is in Heaven." This is success!

Home

Our Heavenly Home is in our Heart.

Heart is Where Our Home Is

I carry my home wherever I go
It's in my heart where I feel love flow
Whenever I need a place to hide
I just stop to be and go inside

Warm loving energy of Great Spirit
Comforts my being, I'm always near it
Wisdom speaks as I hush my mind
Whatever I need is what I find

Blessings of love to feel and to give
Makes my life joyous as I live
Knowing home as the place we blend
Divine harmony brings truth to mend

Although I've had my share of pain
A deeper love have I gained
Layers peeled of what isn't true
Leaving pure love to give to you

Being home grants opportunity
To feel God's love and our unity
Inside each heart is our great home
The one that we have always known

God of My Heart

Have you ever felt homesick? Have you ever felt uncomfortable, unhappy, or insecure being where you are? Our true home is in the heaven of our heart. We take it with us wherever we go.

In the Wizard of Oz, when Dorothy clicked her ruby slippers together, she closed her eyes and focused her concentration inside and recited three times: "There's no place like home."

Our hearts are our home. Inside, we are guided by our feelings. Our personal Star of Bethlehem, where our light shines eternally, is leading us Home, where we feel the true essence of ourselves, love. It is God that exists in our hearts. It is that spark of God that is the essence of who we truly are. When we deny or repress our feelings, we are denying God's messages. Feelings are conscious energy. When we sit with them, they exude inner wisdom.

Emotions are stuck energy that we release as we experience the events of our lives. On our journey homeward, toward the full expression of our Eternal Self, we are letting go of old negative feelings, or repressed energy. We are actually transmuting them with the fire of love from our hearts and using the energy to create a new life and world based on real reality. We are giving ourselves compassion for our difficult life experiences and at the same time listening for the lessons and insights.

Our connection to the God and to each other is right inside our hearts. When we place our attention in our hearts with an open mind, we feel loved and comforted. We hear our still, small voice within. We learn about ourselves.

The more we listen to our feelings and follow their guidance, the closer we feel to Home. Home is peaceful and loving. Home is where we find understanding of ourselves and of Life.

During these times of rapid change and transformation, it is beneficial to go Home often. No matter what is happening in our life or world, we can find comfort, wisdom, love, power, and solace inside our hearts. We know when we are Home, no matter what is happening in the outside world, all is well. We know that because deep inside, we know that Life is eternal. Nothing can harm our Eternal Selves.

God gives us guidance whenever we ask. Everything we need is found within the Home of our hearts. Everything.

Anything that doesn't feel like love can be transmuted back into love by taking it into our hearts. Any problem we may have will find its solution in the home of our hearts.

We are Home with God and each other in our hearts. Through our heart connection, we know we are family. In our New World we live together in the same Home. It's a place of peace, understanding, and love.

Paradise

Take time to imagine our
peaceful paradise on Earth.

Welcome to Paradise.
After all, it _is_ a New World!

Peaceful Paradise

Ahh! We're in heaven on earth that's for sure
Like the energy in nature, it seems so pure
Take a deep breath; it seems so refreshing
We're living in harmony, all energies meshing

Now everyone loves and gets love in return
We're living in peace; the tables have turned
We don't have to do anything, we can just be
We love each other unconditionally

We've all worked so hard to discard our old stuff
We said: "no more misery, we've had enough!"
Nobody stands for anything except for the truth
The whole world is free, even our youth

Greed is absolved; we all have enough
All tummies are full; no more times that are tough
We play and enjoy our unique creativity
We've opened up to our inner sensitivity

The truth has revealed a great understanding
The love within unity and awareness expanding
No more secrets or lies, pollution or war
We've peeled all the layers and reached the core

At last each Inner Child has been freed
Our Father-Mother God meets every need
We experience the Oneness of God's presence
We've realized the purity of our very essence

We've ushered in a new age of peace
With love we've helped our joy to increase
With bright sunny days and feelings so light
We celebrate life all day and all night

Peaceful Living

It is time to live in peace. We are at a place within our own selves, where the passion for peace is so deep, it compels us to **make peace happen**.

Our primary challenge is to create a lasting peace within ourselves. We are becoming more accepting of "what is" and we are releasing the old patterns of resistance. We are accepting our feelings. We are accepting each other, and we are accepting and honoring each other's feelings as being truth. No more arguments, no more internal or personal wars. Feelings are what they are, and they represent personal truth. There is no right or wrong with feelings. We each have a right to our own truth. With our common intent to accept and understand feelings, we are finding peace.

Our feelings are showing us how to find peace in our lives. When we express our feelings openly and honestly, we understand each other and find ways to compromise.

We are gravitating toward people who resonate with us. These people accept us the way we are. They are open to honest communication. We are free to be ourselves and we allow them to be the freedom to be who they are.

One primary solution we are finding is to process feelings of discord within ourselves rather than run negative energy at other people, such as anger. We learn what our feelings mean to us by being present with them inside. With acceptance and compassion for our own feelings, we understand ourselves enough to communicate in a peaceful manner. We are changing negative reactions to communication about what we want or stand for. The nature of our communication may be gentle or passionate, but when it comes from love and not hate or fear, it feels good to hear the truth, even if it is not in alignment with what we want. We accept truth and live in peace.

Competition, greed, and anger disrupt our peace. When we find these energies within, we are processing them. We release the old egoic patterns. Instead of being reactive, we are being responsible. We are responding with the intent to be understood. We are listening with the intent to understand. We are using the energy of love to be cooperative.

The energy of competition attempts to separate the inseparable, or feed illusions of separateness or superiority. When people buy these illusions, they destroy relationships, personal or business. People now embrace unity and inclusion, and love and cooperation are prevalent. Relationships are stronger. Groups are forming. This creates the peace we long for. We get much more than that—we get a sense of security that money can't buy.

Greed comes from an illusion based on material values. We now have established love based value systems that promote generosity and community. We now share openly. We know there's more where that came from.

We let anger show us what our boundaries are, then we use the energy to stand our ground. We don't accept unkind or cruel treatment because we love and value ourselves. We know we don't have to take any kind of abuse, physically, verbally, or emotionally.

As we focus our attention on peace, we stay centered on our pivotal place of peace within and remain poised. We let people be who they are, but we don't let them create drama in our lives. We give our attention to those around us who can be peaceful, and we are distancing from people who just don't get it yet, or who don't treat us well.

We are earnestly working toward peace. We are creating peace within, peace in our lives, peace in our families, peace with our friends, and peace in our world. We are living in peaceful, cooperative communities. We are bound and determined to vote for politicians who will actively create peace among the nations of the world.

People are demonstrating for peace all around the world. We are uniting. We are demanding peace.

Let's celebrate Peace now. Make it so in our hearts and minds, in unison, in the now moment. Feel it deeply and maintain the feeling. As we feel and envision peace together in our New World, we are expanding the Pure Energy of Heaven in our hearts to our outer world on Earth. Glory to God for this gift.

Hope

When we have planted the seed of hope, which grows into faith,
within every person who walks the planet, then our global
healing will have truly begun.
Until then, we have much work to do.

Believe in Hope

Though our problems have a purpose and improve us in the end
We suffer from our afflictions and need God as a friend
Our Lord who keeps His promises leaves us this anticipation
That through belief in His word our misery meets termination

Though we see no cessation in view—it is our belief we embrace
For such is the nature of hope: the future does not show its face
With hope in our heart we increase endurance to patiently wait
And in the interim we learn perseverance fortifies our faith

So we find one magnifies the other and both hope and faith abound
It is the most amazing strength faith consequently found
To our dear Lord who gave us these through His great love for us
We feel our gratitude deeply and in Him our lives we trust

How to Inspire Hope

Sometimes when we feel down, sad or discouraged, we need to get in touch with our faith to shine a ray of hope. Friends remind us of Biblical truths such as: "this too shall pass", or "the Lord never gives us more than we can handle," or they remind us how much we are loved.

Inside we have our own resources for inspiring hope. When we feel challenged, we often go in and say: "Ok, I surrender, God. Show me my lesson. What is the answer to my challenge?" We get answers. We feel something inside of us start to move. We release our situation and feelings to God. Things change. We get a phone call. We pick up a book and we find answers to our present challenge. Something happens.

God works through our own hearts, and also people, too. God inspires us to help others and to offer hope. Just being available to someone in need is a Source of great support. We put ourselves in position to answer a cry for help by being there for them, whether in conversation or in person. Ideas surface. We find ways to lighten the moment. We point out the positive aspects of our friend's life. We point out their positive qualities.

Changes in our lives offer opportunities to grow in another direction. Sometimes challenges are our call for change. We bear losses. We find we have created empty spaces in our lives. The void sometimes leaves a feeling of sadness or fear.

Voids don't last forever. They are just spaces that are made to be filled by our next step in life. Life flows. There is nothing to fear. Faith is believing that God really does supply every need. Even when we don't know how that need will be fulfilled, or how we will get through some situation, when we rely on our faith and know that a void just means something new is on the way, then we have hope.

Pointing out the truth inspires hope. The truth is, we are all loved and cared for. The truth is, we are all equal, yet unique. We each are needed in this world. The moment we lose our self and help another, we find our True Self because we realize our connection. We inspire hope in ourselves by helping another.

We are not alone, ever. We have Guardian angels and other beings on different realms, including our family and friends who have passed on. Life is eternal. The more we acknowledge beings that are not in a physical body, the more we realize that we have all the help we need.

God doesn't have a body, and yet is in all bodies. When we pray to the God of our heart, and know we are eternally connected to all beings, miracles happen!

When we remind each other to check in with our hearts and pray, we inspire hope. We know that truth and faith abide within. We get inspired with creative solutions by directing our feelings and questions into our heart.

Our very experiences of life demonstrate that there are many caring people in the world who serve as the arms of God ready to take position to answer our cries for help. We are all serving God in our own way. God serves us, too, and will never abandon us in a time of need.

In our New World, we are dependably there for each other to inspire hope. Our hope always leads us to faith. We know each passing situation or event carries its own perfection in the end, which is always a new beginning.

Faith

Faith is the muscle whose strength,
when exercised through daily application of living truth,
gives us the confidence to face life with ease.

The Power of Faith

I choose my beliefs with unlimited power
As I trust in God in every hour
The feeling I get inside as I pray
Illumines my Self and brightens my way

My consciousness shifts and expands who I AM
I become attuned to God's Divine plan
All concern is replaced with Unconditional Love
Now I see Life is perfect, it's below as above

All of the circumstances I experience in life
Whether those of joy or those of strife
Are blessings of love chosen by me
I love myself, too, unconditionally

I feel God's love, in that I am basking
I get what I want just for the asking
Carefully attuned to the Will of God
With ease and joy in life I trod

Whenever fear or doubt sneaks in
I turn to God; I always win
Ever-brighter I shine the rays of my star
As I blend with God, that's very far!

Surrender to Our Trustworthy God

Why are we ever shy about speaking to God? Why do we ever feel unworthy, or shameful, or guilty and feel that God might not like us? It's because sometimes we attribute human love to God. We learn about love from other humans who in their humanness sometimes withdraw their display or words of love. They criticize us for our perceived faults, and somehow we feel unlovable. We even condemn ourselves sometimes.

God loves us no matter what. There is not one thing we can say, think, or do that diminishes God's love for us. Pure unconditional love is our birthright. It is always available. In any moment we can stop, be still, place our attention on God in our hearts and feel loved. The more we practice and focus, the more we feel it.

We are growing to love ourselves unconditionally, too. Even though we become aware of things we want to change, we can still love ourselves "as is" as God does. God understands us totally, even when we don't understand ourselves.

We really are just innocent children. That's what humanness is. We have an internal conscience that tells us if we are doing right or wrong, which is really whether we are behaving out of love or not. This is our guidance. It is not meant to shame us into withdrawal from God. It is a gift.

Even when we are experiencing our karmic lessons, we can lessen our load and expedite the process by asking for the lesson and for the burden to be removed. We can always trust God to help.

The more we lean on God, the more God strengthens us. Our faith grows the more we rely on it.

We are expected to develop our own powers of intelligence, feeling, and will. God gave us free will to be able to experience anything we desire. We are not judged for having any desire. God let's us experience things so that we can learn about everything. There is no good or bad, right or wrong. We are like little children who are spiritual scientists. We just want to know "What's this like?"

Knowingness creates experience. When we practice this truth: "Be still and know that I am God," we claim our Oneness with God. We feel the love and power of God. As we commune with God we co-create the manifestation of our desires into our outer physical reality. Knowing that we are made in His and Her likeness and image, we feel our own inherent creative powers. By envisioning our desires in this state of consciousness with a feeling of gratitude, miracles occur. We manifest our desires rapidly.

When we tire of chasing desires that lead to temporary or false happiness, we surrender to the Will of God. We follow the joy in our heart. We give up human beliefs and believe in God, the only true power of limitless possibilities.

No matter what circumstance we find ourselves in, whether it seems dire as in divorce, loss of a child or loved one, or a loss of material wealth, or an everyday circumstance, we can dive into our innermost being and find God, our Great Comforter and Provider. With implicit faith in God, we are raised up in consciousness. We become grateful for what we have. We sense a new deeper feeling of abundance. This shift in consciousness, when practiced, leads to a renewed sense of abundance on every level. Our outer life reflects God's love through others. We experience miracles. We receive material wealth. To the extent we trust God to deliver, we can receive.

One helpful hint is to withdraw attention from "naysayers." Withdraw attention from the reality of the outside world. Forget about statistics, what's probable, or the way things appear. After all, the outside world is just a reflection of previous thoughts. By changing our thoughts to what we do want to experience, and directly telling God what we desire, we will change our outer experience. This is what is thought of as miraculous. The improbable becomes reality by methods unknown to man. This practice builds and strengthens faith.

Practice God's presence whether alone or among others. Know that God is present in everyone and everything. See God's good everywhere with a feeling of gratitude. Practice having confidence in God. We can never ask for too much, but by releasing old habits and desires and attuning to the Will of God, simplicity enters our life and we feel deeply fulfilled, at peace within—independent of outside circumstances—and our inner joy is illumined.

In our New World, we surrender to God in full faith and trust. We feel light and free. We claim our Divine birthright of an inner feeling of abundance. We open to creative ideas and inspiration. We become a light of the world and a benefit to others. We live in joy.

God

Love God as Life.
Live life as love.

"Listen now, how as a result of proper study and practice, with the attention anchored in God, you can know the fullness of Reality without doubt."

Krishna
The Bhagavad Gita

I See You, God

In you, dear friend, I see what's good
You can do things that I never could
You express love uniquely as you do
There's not another soul exactly like you

I see you, God, shining through my friend
I see you peeking with a hand to lend
I know you're there in those squeezy hugs
I feel the bond as my heart tugs

I see you God, in children's laughter
Reminding me of joy I'm after
I feel you God, as I play
I feel you in my life that way

I hear you God, as I listen inside
With your love my tears have dried
Your wisdom wells up in my mind
Teaching me always to be kind

I feel you God, as warmth in my heart
I sense your guidance as I play my part
I treasure you God, as the human race
I see you shine in every face

I love you God, you are my soul
We are One, truth be told
I am you God, as I love my friend
The cycle is complete but will never end

Dedicated to God in all of us!

Love God

"Devotion, love for God,
is the magnetic attraction of the heart that God cannot resist."

Paramahansa Yogananda
"Prayer is the Soul's Sincere Desire"
Self Realization Fellowship Worldwide Prayer Circle

God is always present, whether we place our attention on Him and Her or not. God's love is everywhere. By concentrating on God's presence, we can feel God's love. Like a parent, we can touch God's heart with our sincere, childlike love. Our prayers of devotion deepen our relationship with God.

When we love God, we feel very close to Him. She responds with a deep feeling of love returned. God feels joy. We feel nurtured in the deepest sense. We experience our Oneness. We satisfy our soul.

It is in this space of total concentration on God that we know within the depths of our being that we are deeply loved unconditionally. God understands our feelings—our frustrations, our concerns, and all of our desires. When we take them to God, we begin to understand ourselves more. We become aware of the perfection and purpose of our lives. We understand that we are worthy of unconditional love. We develop unconditional love for ourselves.

When we practice loving ourselves unconditionally, we grow the God-spark within us. We eliminate negative self-talk. We appreciate our own inner beauty. We are inspired to be the best we can be, and more.

In loving ourselves, we are loving God. We illuminate our True Selves and begin to shine radiantly. God already sees us as our potential. He and she understand the natural process of maturing souls. God is always there to help us in every way. The more we ask for help, the more we receive it. Whenever we feel we don't have enough, that's just evidence that we haven't asked for enough.

As we commune with God, we also come to understand God more. We increase our awareness of God's presence in all things. We feel God's kiss in the wind. We see God's beauty in nature. We know that all love, no matter the delivery method, is from God. We lose attachments to particular people, places, or circumstances. We know God will find a way to love us no matter who we are with, no matter where we are, and no matter what our life circumstances are.

We see the good in others as God. As we love the good in them, we are loving God. We pay less attention to their human acts of non-love and focus on their good qualities. We see them as perfect as God does.

God loves us. The more we focus on this thought and get present in God's love, the more life responds. It is simply miraculous.

In our New World, we are fully aware that God loves us, and we love God.

Epilogue

I'm finding my experience of this New World to be one of great love and gratitude to Life. As I continually practice applying the wisdom of love, the living truth, I feel so free just to be my Self. I love getting reminders from my friends and family of the truths that we are incorporating into our way of being. It helps to anchor the awareness into beingness. By managing my personal energy efficiently with conscious direction of my attention, I'm becoming more adept at receiving Divine Grace and Love into my inner world and expressing it in my outer world. I have much to learn and improve upon.

I know in my heart that unconditional love and acceptance is changing the world. Everyone is doing the best they can, according to their level of understanding in each moment. I intend to love the good in everyone and to remember we all have God/good in us—otherwise we wouldn't even be alive. I especially appreciate those who live in integrity; whose words and actions are in alignment. And I really feel blessed and full of deep gratitude to those who consistently act with kindness.

As we each create a new inner world of peace and self-love, we realize in our Oneness of Spirit that we are transforming the world. We are now serving the masses by cooperating in the manifestation of a planetary shift—reflecting our internal shift in consciousness—as we each share our unique gifts. Each one of us is needed for our unique contribution to the world. As we emerge with awakened awareness into this new paradigm of reality, we have become empowered as conscious co-creators with God to use our love energy to transform destructive energies and experiences to new constructive energies and joyful experiences. As we listen and follow our inner guidance, and really love God, our Selves, and each other, we are helping to manifest the Divine Plan of bringing Heaven to Earth.

There is hope for our planet. All of the external results of previous mis-creations can change in the wink of an eye. Focus on the good in the world. Focus on the good in your self. Focus on the good in others. Focus on solutions. Make the expression of love your highest priority.

Just know that we are tuned in to God and to each other in our hearts. When we pray to God for help, others come to our aid as God inspires them. We are inspired by God to become the answers to the prayers of others. We answer each other's prayers, hopes, and dreams by tuning in to our hearts and loving God. We are the love of God made manifest.

Never doubt the goodness of Life. Regardless of outer circumstances in the world, realize there is no power greater than the love from which life emanates. Keep the faith in the only power that lasts. With your attention focused on the Divine, you will see first in inner perception, then globally in outer reality, the miraculous transformation of our planet Earth. Stay tuned!

Blessings of love, Michelle

The End

...is only the Beginning

When you open your heart!